"...the reader finds himself deeply grateful that Miss Buck is a writer who always manages to say 'yes' to life."

—Los Angeles *Times*

Readers who remember with pleasure Pearl S. Buck's autobiographical **MY SEVERAL WORLDS** will find in this new volume a continuation of her experiences and of her personal reflections on a constantly changing and eventful life.

With candor and humility she shares the intimate thoughts that pressed in upon her relentlessly in the long wakeful nights as she struggled to accept the death of her husband and to adjust to her new life alone.

A BRIDGE FOR PASSING will be read with deep emotion as a testament of faith by a woman whose memories of a happy life helped her gallantly and successfully to cross the bridge from sorrow to serenity.

A BRIDGE FOR PASSING was originally published by the John Day Company.

Other books by Pearl S. Buck

**The Angry Wife*
**Come, My Beloved*
**Command the Morning*
**The Good Earth*
†Hearts Come Home and Other Stories
†Imperial Woman
**Letter from Peking*
**The Strong Love*
†My Several Worlds
**Pavilion of Women*
**Peony*
**Portrait of a Marriage*
**Satan Never Sleeps*
†The Townsman

*Published in *Cardinal* editions.
†Published in *Giant Cardinal* editions.

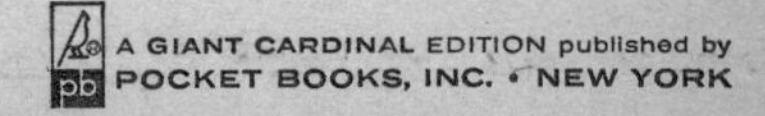
A GIANT CARDINAL EDITION published by
POCKET BOOKS, INC. • NEW YORK

A BRIDGE FOR PASSING

John Day edition published April, 1962
A **Giant Cardinal** edition
1st printing .... July, 1963

This *Giant Cardinal*** edition includes every word contained in the original, higher-priced edition. It is printed from brand-new plates made from completely reset, clear, easy-to-read type. *Giant Cardinal* editions are published by Pocket Books, Inc., and are printed and distributed in the U.S.A. by Affiliated Publishers, a division of Pocket Books, Inc., 630 Fifth Avenue, New York 20, N.Y.
*Trademark registered in the United States and other countries.
**Trademark of Pocket Books, Inc., 630 Fifth Avenue, New York 20, N.Y., in the United States and other countries.

L

This **Giant Cardinal** edition is published by arrangement with The John Day Company, Inc.
Printed in the U.S.A.

It is as it is

MOTTO OF EDWARD III, 1340 A.D.

What, then, is to be done?
I take refuge in my heart,
where I love him as I wish.

PAUL VALERY

A BRIDGE FOR PASSING

One

I REMEMBER THE DAY when I decided to make the picture in Japan, an April day a year ago, a day like this one upon which I begin the story of my return to Asia. I have always known that the return was inevitable, not a permanent return, for I am too happy in my country to live elsewhere, but a return, nevertheless. One does not live half a life in Asia without return. When it would be I did not know, nor even where it would be, or for what cause. In our changing world nothing changes more than geography. The friendly country of China, the home of my childhood and youth, is for the time being forbidden country. I refuse to call it enemy country. The people in my memory are too kind and the land too beautiful.

China is not the whole of Asia, however, in spite of being most of it. There are other countries to which I could return—Japan, India, Korea and all the rest. Japan, I suppose, is the one I know best after China. Logically, the return would be there, but when? I am not a tourist. I do not enjoy visiting a country merely to see the sights. Nor do I enjoy visiting as a special person. When I return to Japan, I told myself, it will be for a project, a piece of work, something interesting to do, something that will explain why I cannot accept all the dinner invitations, weekends, entertainments which hospitable people offer to friends. But what project? A new question was added to my where and when.

Quite unexpectedly one day it was proposed to me that I go to Japan to work with others on the filming of my book, *The Big Wave.* The work would be something new and therefore exciting. I am long past the conservatism and caution of youth. I have arrived at the adventuresome age and *The Big Wave* is an adventurous book. It involves a remote fishing village, a tidal wave, a volcano, none of which I had seen for decades, and which I hankered to see again. The questions were answered. As to where, it was Japan; as to when, it was now.

No, not quite answered, for there was my family to consider. Some of them were old and some very young, a large family spreading over generations and into ramifications. Could I, should I, leave them all at such a time? We went into family consultation. Apparently I could and should. The family doctor assured me that there was no reason to delay going. The children, grown and half grown, were hearty and healthy. And he? He was as he ever would be always now. If I waited for the final possibility, it might be years. Six months ago I could not have left him. But in the brief interval there was for me all the difference between day and night. He had slipped into a world of his own. I had not yet learned to bear what was and must ever be.

"Go," the doctor said. "You must have a change. You have a long road ahead."

"Go," my responsible daughter said. "I will look after everything."

Thus encouraged, contracts were signed and tickets bought.

The book, of course, had to be put into new form. *The Big Wave* is a simple story but its subject is huge. It deals with life and death and life again through a handful of human beings in a remote fishing village on the southern tip of the lovely island of Kyushu in the south of Japan. The book has always had a vigorous life of its own. It has won some awards in its field, it has been translated into many languages, but never into the strange and wonderful language of the motion picture. To use that language was in itself adventure, not words now, but human beings, moving, talking, dying with courage, living and loving with even greater courage. I am accustomed to the usual arts. I have made myself familiar with canvas and brush, with clay and stone, with instruments of music, but the motion picture is different from all these. Yet it, too, is a great art. Even when it is desecrated by cheap people and cheap material, the medium is inspiring in its potential. When artists are great enough, we shall have many great pictures. I was not under the illusion of greatness but I hoped that we could make a picture true to the people of whom I had written.

We set forth on a morning in May. Japan had been a near neighbor all during my years in China. When I was a child, if we sailed from Vancouver or San Francisco, then Japan was the last stop before Shanghai, the gateway to my Chinese home. If we sailed from Shanghai, then Japan was the first stop toward my American home. It had been, too, a country of refuge when revolutionary wars drove us out of China. I once spent many months in a small Japanese house in the mountains near Unzen, and Unzen is near the southern part of the island of Kyushu, near Obama. I had taken a motor trip in that same year around Kyushu, and had stopped briefly in Obama to bathe in the hot springs there. In mind I now saw my fishing village somewhere in that region of glorious seacoast, green mountains and smoking volcano.

"I shall recognize it the moment I see it," I told my family. "It will be a little village hugging a rocky shore, a sandy cove between mountains, a few houses of stone behind a high sea wall. I see it as though I remembered it, although I do not know its name."

If Japan had been near and familiar in the past, this time it seemed just outside the gates of my home in Pennsylvania. We entered a jet in New York, two hours or so away from my stone farmhouse, and were airborne in a matter of minutes. I reflected upon the incredible span of my life. Though, God willing, I have decades more to live upon this beautiful globe, yet in experience of life and peoples, I began in the middle ages. As a child I traveled by wheelbarrow, sedan chair, mule cart or in a boat pulled along a lazy canal by men walking the towpath. I was twelve years old before I saw a railway train in China and fifteen before I rode in it. Ships I knew, for there were ships on the Yangtze River to take us to Shanghai and thence across the Pacific or up the river to Kiukiang and the mountains of Lu, where we escaped the torrid summer heat of the plains. I did not see or ride in an automobile until I was in college and after that not again for years until I returned to live in my own country. Then I became a modern woman and traveled by air as a matter of course. No, wait—I once took a disheveled little airplane to shorten a journey to Rangoon. Otherwise it would have been a matter of eight days on a slow boat. And once I flew from Sweden to Copenhagen on another journey. Yes, and still again, I flew from Ceylon to Java, descending once into the wet jungle heat of Sumatra. Years later, my first trip by jet was in Europe in the incredibly swift and silent jet aircraft that flies between Copenhagen and Rome. My interest in science has kept my curiosity keen in the development of jet and rocket, and anything slower than a jet makes me impatient now—I who began my life at a speed no greater than four miles an hour by sedan chair!

When the jet lifted me from the earth to the sky that May morning in New York I confess, however, to an elation all but unique. The huge metallic bird girded itself for flight, its engines roared, the creature trembled with its own inner power. Part of the elation was perhaps a reckless awareness of my own complete helplessness as we soared into the upper air. I had committed myself to the machine. I could not escape, I could not descend. No decisions faced me, for there was no way to go but up. An old Chinese proverb says that of the thirty-six ways of escape, the best is to run away. I do not know what the other thirty-five ways are—curiously enough, I never thought to inquire in all those years in China, I suppose because the obvious answer would have been that they were unnecessary, since one can always run away. This is no longer true, however, in our modern age. When one commits one's self to an airborne craft and the door is fastened against earth and home, there is no escape even by running away. The result is a strange sense of peace —desperate, perhaps, but peace.

Such random thoughts fluttered through my mind that morning while through the tiny window I watched the globe circle away from me. When—and if—I returned to it hours later, the wide continent of my native land and the blue stretch of the Pacific Ocean would be between me and home, although in my childhood our ship took weeks to cross that same ocean and our train another week to cross the continent. Yet this new world has never seemed strange to me. Speed has become a matter of course as well as of necessity. We floated over a sea of silvery clouds, and I settled back in my chair to work on the script of my picture.

The Hawaiian Islands are stepping stones between Asia and the United States. I remember them as islands of hope when I was a child and traveled in ships. Ten days from San Francisco to Honolulu or eight days from Yokohama to Honolulu was the expectation. But eastward or west, I was always eager to reach the islands of eternal green, where coconuts could be had for the picking and garlands of fragrant flowers were everyday greetings. Speed of aircraft has deprived us of something of the excitement of the great ship easing into dock after the long voyage and the sight of crowds of friends waiting, or even the sadness of the last moments of farewell, and friends waving from the dock as the great ship pulls its anchors aweigh for the long voyage ahead.

In our jet aircraft we came down smartly and sharply in Honolulu, not a moment late, and were met by efficient persons and taken to our hotel for the night. I had decided on the stop, not only because I wanted to see Honolulu again but particularly because I wanted to drive once more along the jagged mountains behind the city. I wanted to sees the surfboard riders glide in on the waves. Above all, I wanted to feel the atmosphere of Hawaii as a free state now in a free nation. I had a fancy that to belong to a nation, as an integral part, must mean subsidence of island discontents and grumblings—not that there was ever much grumbling in Hawaii, where the air is always warm and rain and sun fall daily on the just and the unjust alike and often at the same time. No, it would be a matter of spirit.

It was night when we came down and the moon shone on the white surf and the dark sea. The hotel was a royal one and as we crossed the immense lobby to claim our rooms and settle ourselves for sleep, men and women were still coming and going, people of various races and costumes. None was strange to me except the women tourists in Mother Hubbards, those garments devised by sensitive missionaries in the early days when, like Adam and Eve in their Eden, the Hawaiians did not know they were naked. The missionaries knew, of course, and enjoying the vagaries and waywardness of the human heart, I have sometimes wondered whether it was the early missionary men who commanded the lovely naked women to be covered, lest saints yield to the devil within us all, or whether it was the missionary women in their long skirts and sleeves and high collars who knew they could never compete with the smooth brown bodies wearing nothing except a gay bit of cloth or wisp of grass about their loins and a red flower in their waving black hair. Only God knows, and He keeps such secrets to Himself—with a smile, perhaps! Today by the whimsy of fashion the girls of Hawaii wear smart western clothes and the tourists wear flowing Mother Hubbards and again the Hawaiian women have the best of it.

The air of Hawaii is divine, no less. I lay in my comfortable bed and slept and woke to breathe in the soft pure atmosphere blown in by a gentle wind from the sea and slept again until the sun was flaming into my room. I rose then and bathed and dressed and breakfasted alone on the small terrace outside my room. The outside air was exactly that of my own body. I felt no break into heat or cold. So an unborn child must feel the sheltering waters of its first home. It is an indescribably smooth fluidity and the result is well-being, a total absence of conflict with environment.

Already there were surf riders enjoying the morning swell of the waves, and men and women in all but nothing were sauntering on the beach. And I was quite right about the spiritual change. The waiter who brought my breakfast moved with a calm and a confidence which signified an inner content. We conversed briefly on the subject after I had remarked that when I visited Honolulu before it had not been the capital of a state.

"Everything is better now," he told me.

"How is it better?" I asked.

He shrugged expressive shoulders. "It is not a question of food or clothes or anything to hold in the hands. It is just—better altogether. Now we are belonging. Now we can speak. . . . Madame, the marmalade is very good—fresh orange, fresh pineapple. I advise!"

"Thank you," I said, "and I think you are right. Everything is better."

I reflected upon this wisdom after he had broken my egg into the cup and poured my coffee and had gone away. Exclusion is always dangerous. Inclusion is the only safety if we are to have a peaceful world, inclusion in a national commonwealth, inclusion into an international commonwealth of nations. I believe that every nation should belong to the United Nations as inescapably and irrevocably as a child is born into a family. Resignation should be impossible. If, in a fit of pettishness, the child withdraws or even runs away, he is still a member of the family. The basic relationship applies on a world scale to the family of nations. Anything basic is simple and comprehensive. It is only the simple that can be large enough to comprehend all confusions.

I do not love surfboard riding. The sea and I are not enemies, but we are, let us say, wary friends. I have had encounters with an angry sea, and even with a friendly sea, friendly in the way that a lion can be friendly, felling a man with a playful pat.

Once, on an August day in Martha's Vineyard, he and

I were swimming in the surf. There had been a storm a few days before and though the sky was blue that morning, the sea was rolling in on magnificent waves.

"Take my hand," he said, "we'll be strong enough together."

We were not strong enough, even together. The sea caught us in its huge paws, we were swept off our feet, swept out and out until we were choking and blinded and half drowned. Still hand in hand, we were thrown down at last upon the sand and so escaped. What I remember was the total helplessness of those moments in the wave, when we were at the merciless disposal of insensate power. We walked up the beach in silence, he and I, grateful for life and wanting no more of the sea that day.

I had no inclination, therefore, to go surfboarding alone in Honolulu.

Nor is it any use for me to imagine that I can enjoy myself in a crowd. Autograph hunters are everywhere in the world, and not liking to appear ungracious, it is best for me to be solitary. Alone, therefore, I enjoyed my terrace and the view of sea and mountain. I read the local newspapers, always an aid to understanding, and let the day slip past me until luncheon with friends and a drive in an open Jeep around the islands. Waikiki is for tourists, and it is only when one leaves it that one sees the other beaches, sheltered in coves, where the people who live in Honolulu, or nearby, gather their families to play and picnic. The road is excellent and it hugs a gorgeous shoreline. We stopped often as we drove to watch the crash of heavy surf against the black rocks of ancient lava and again, as in so many times in my life, I lingered to marvel and to admire the strange steep cliffs of those dark and abrupt mountains facing the sea. It is incredible that human beings could climb those upright shafts of lava rock, or that there are caves and crevices between them. Yet men in other ages have so climbed and into the caves and crevices they carried canoes and boats to become the tombs of their famous sea captains. Today other men climb to bring down the vessels again and clean them of ancient dust and put them into museums. I was reminded of Norway and the great ships in museums there which also were the tombs of the men of the sea. Here in Hawaii the feat seems incredible because of the smooth steepness of the clifflike mountains.

It was dark when we went back to the hotel and the evening newspaper carried headlines of a vast earthquake in Chile. I read of the disaster and grieved for those whose lives were lost.

Chile! I remembered that the Downwind Expedition of the recent International Geophysical Year had carried by ship, in its Pacific under-ocean exploration, a device that, bound to the ocean floor, could measure the heat flow from inner earth to the Pacific floor. On the Easter Island rise the heat flow increased sharply. Easter Island and Sala y Gomez, both Chilean, are the result of this rise. And just off the western coast of Chile itself there is a long deep trench, its bottom sharply narrow, a compensation for the Andes, but produced probably by a creeping river of cold material flowing out from the center of the ocean and pushing its way under the rocky continental mass. A strange silent underworld, this ocean bed, a violent world when catastrophe takes place in the conflict between fire and water, heat and cold.

Chile seemed far away from the pleasant islands of Hawaii and I turned to the demands of the evening. We were to have dinner in the night club across the street, and thither we went to enjoy Hawaiian food and music and dances. The dances made me laugh again and again. They were not only beautiful—they were also subtle and gay, satires on life. One dance, given ostensibly in memory of the first missionaries, was especially humorous. A lovely slender brown girl came on the stage. She wore a white old-fashioned western dress of embroidered muslin, not a Mother Hubbard but the sort of dress the wife of a missionary might have worn a hundred years ago, high neck, long sleeves, narrowed at the waist, full-skirted to the floor with a ruffled train. The girl was the picture of sweet innocence, her long black hair smoothly combed into a knot at her nape. The only touch of color, except her full red lips, was a scarlet hibiscus flower behind her left ear and this flower made me suspicious. In a few minutes my suspicions were confirmed and I was in helpless laughter. For this girl, this innocent island maiden, enveloped from head to foot in white, performed a dance so fraught with all the wiles of woman enticing man that Eve herself, had she seen it, would have wanted lessons. Within the white encasement the beautiful brown body curved and quivered in sensual joy, not primitive, for such joy is eternal, renewing itself in every generation of man and woman, a dance of love.

The subdued light of the lanterns fell on the circle of watching faces, each absorbed in its own dream, its private memory or unfulfilled desire. When it was over there was silence, a long sigh, then thunderous applause. The lovely girl smiled and bowed and went away and though we clapped until our palms burned, she would not return.

The master of ceremonies had prefaced each event with a pleasant rattle of conversation and several times during the evening he had mentioned a tidal wave. He had said, tossing it off as a joke, that perhaps we would all enjoy the excitement of a tidal wave and therefore he had ordered one as an added attraction for the evening. None of us took this seriously until now as we woke again to reality, and he began to prattle again of the tidal wave. Suddenly I heard sharply and clearly what he said. He was not announcing a tidal wave, he was warning us of its approach.

I rose at once with my companion and left the room and crossed the street to the hotel. There all was confusion. Guests were being sent to the upper floors and streets facing the sea were barricaded. What to do! We looked at one another in consternation. Our jet was scheduled to fly at an hour after midnight. It was now just short of eleven o'clock. If life and its crises have taught me anything it is to proceed with the schedule until it becomes impossible. We proceeded by rushing to our rooms, packing our bags and taking the last available taxicab to the airport.

The airport in Honolulu, as everyone knows, is on a narrow peninsula of land just above sea level. When we arrived it was alarmingly empty. A few employees stood staring at the horizon and the cabman was in haste to be paid off. In a few minutes we found ourselves alone in the big waiting room, and were escorted by a gloomy attendant to an upper floor and a comfortable club room, empty except for a frightened hostess behind the lunch counter. She welcomed us without enthusiasm, poured coffee and then walked to the big window and stared into the darkness over the sea. We sat down on the couch and listened, perforce, to the blaring of the radio fixed into the ceiling above our heads. It was playing jazz but every other moment or two the music broke and an inexorable voice announced that the tidal wave had reached another island and that the height was mounting. In a few minutes it would strike Hilo at an estimated height of over sixty feet. We also learned that the wave was a result of the earthquake in Chile. There is a continental connection under the ocean between that deep trench off Chile and the islands of the Pacific. Strange symbolism this, by which an earthquake in one hemisphere produces a tidal wave in the other!

My meditation was interrupted by the sudden disappearance of the hostess. She had returned to the counter, murmuring something about her husband and three children. Would they be alarmed when she did not come home at midnight as usual? We could not answer her question and neither could she and without another word, even so much as good-by or good night, she left us and was not to be seen again.

We sat on in the vast room. Jazz faded away at midnight and there was only the voice, announcing the onrushing tidal wave. We considered our fate, whatever it was to be, and conversation ceased. Aircraft had been removed from the field, the voice told us, and all flights were canceled. Roads to the hotel were closed. The silence over the city was ominous. We became part of the silence. There was nothing to be done except to wait.

Suddenly at one o'clock sharp the door opened. A breathless young man shouted to us to come at once to the airfield. Our jet would take off in the next few minutes. Yes, the luggage was all on. We seized our handbags and tore after him. The jet was there, we were pushed aboard, and faster than I have ever seen a jet rise into the sky we rose. At exactly the moment we left the earth the radio announced the arrival of the tidal wave.

Mounting into the sky, I was reminded of death itself. The hours of anxiety preceding, the final instant of departure, the inescapable separation from earth and all we had known, the ascent into unknown spaces—is this not the experience of death? There is one difference. From the final flight there is no return. For us there was the hope of return to beautiful Japan.

Yet before we could arrive on earth again, the tidal wave had struck. Rushing through the upper air, we learned by radio that traveling westward, it had already reached Japan. It had traveled more swiftly than our jet to strike with cruel force upon the northeastern shores. The people were warned by the government and could not believe. In their experience, earthquake and tidal wave came as companions. They could not comprehend that an earthquake in Chile might mean a tidal wave on their shores. What strange coincidence, that we were to arrive in Japan at this very moment to make a picture called *The Big Wave!*

"How did you manage it?" the reporters demanded at the airport in Tokyo. "Who is your publicity man?"

They were joking, of course, and we had no publicity man, but it was true that we came riding in upon the publicity of the huge tidal wave. I was grieved that my return to Asia must be upon a storm. I was helpless except to express sympathy for those who had suffered.

I had expected a quiet arrival in Tokyo in other ways. The hour was between two and three after midnight and I could not imagine anyone at the airport to meet me. I thought of one or two business associates, a few friends, perhaps, then a quick ride through dark streets to the old Imperial Hotel, and a bath and bed. It had been a long flight, after all. Sometime in the night we had come down on Wake Island for refueling but it had not seemed important. Outside the window I saw only a cluster of flat buildings and men scurrying here and there, about their business. It might have been anywhere in the middle of the night. Tokyo was another matter.

"I'm glad we are arriving at such a ghastly hour," I had said. "There can't be anyone to meet us."

"Don't be too sure," my companion had retorted.

The great aircraft had trembled as it descended and the lights of Tokyo glittered out of the darkness.

"I am right," I had said. "There is no one here."

A man in a white uniform had stepped forward, "Are you—"

"Yes, we are," I said.

"Then welcome to Japan," he said. "I am with Japan Airlines. This way, please. . . . Just a moment, please . . . photographers and reporters."

We paused. Lights focused us in the darkness and cameras snapped. Reporters crowded around us with questions and exclamations about the tidal wave.

"Thank you," the man said when we showed signs of exhaustion. "Your friends are waiting for you."

Waiting for us? We were speeded through customs, and our friends overwhelmed us indeed with greetings and flowers.

How did I feel? In a way as though I had come home after a long absence and in a way as though I had come to a new and foreign country. The smiling faces, the warm voices, sometimes the eyes brimming with tears, these claimed me for their own. Men and women I had known as young in my own youth were there looking as changed as I do, and with them were children and grandchildren like mine at home, the boys in western clothes, the girls in their formal kimono.

"My daughters rose at one o'clock so that they could wear kimono to welcome you," a friend said proudly.

I know how long it takes to put on kimono properly and make the suitable coiffeur. The girls were beautiful and I was glad they and others wore kimono to make me feel at home when I arrived, at least. When I lived in Japan before the war, all my women friends wore kimono. The most modern and liberal had perhaps one western suit or dress, but this was unusual and not much approved. Now Japanese women wear western dress every day and always except for the few formal occasions of life when they put on their kimono, and many of them own only one kimono and some none at all. There are exceptions, of course. Old women wear kimono and certain distinguished women, even in business, wear kimono always. My special friend wears kimono because it is becoming to her. She has reached the position and the age when she can wear what she likes.

Behind the friendly crowd that night with its flowers and photographers, I was aware of Tokyo itself. I knew how severely it had been bombed in the war, and that now it was rebuilt, new and prosperous, a symbol perhaps of the Japan that was strange to me. Yet even the people who came to greet me seemed changed for the better, I thought. The old stiff formality was somehow gone. I heard ready laughter, not the old polite laughter, but spontaneous and real. Everyone talked freely and without fear. That was new. The sweet courtesy remained, but life and good spirits bubbled through, as though an ancient restraint had been removed. This was my first impression that night, and I shall speak of it again and again because it was expressed everywhere and in many ways.

Meanwhile the photographers were patiently following us at every step. Japanese photographers are indefatigable, philosophical, incredibly agile. They do not demand smiles or pleasant postures. Their cameras click incessantly whereever one is and whatever one is doing. They flew about in the night like fireflies, and we were photographed continuously, embanked in flowers and encircled by friends. We moved en masse at last into waiting cars and were driven at breakneck speed to the Imperial Hotel. I do not know why it is that I have never been terrified by Japanese drivers. They dash through unmarked streets and packed crowds, shouting and warning, and yet they do not have accidents or at least I have not seen accidents. It all seemed natural enough, reminding me of other days, years ago, when I was driven in just such fashion through streets or along the edges of cliffs, up and down mountains or above the sea and roaring surf. Perhaps lack of fear is simply because in Asia I relax into Oriental acceptance and realize there is practically nothing I can do about anything.

We arrived finally and alive at the Imperial Hotel, that haven where Japan meets the world with her own grace and style, combined with an amazing amount of comfort and good service, and an hour later we were asleep in air-conditioned rooms, surrounded by flowers in Japanese baskets.

Yet for a long time I could not sleep. Memory went to work and pictures passed through my mind. The first was the vivid face of my mother, brown hair, brown skin, brown eyes. We were sitting on the wide veranda of our house in China. I was perhaps seven, a barefoot child with long yellow hair, sitting on the floor before her, hugging my knees and listening. She was telling me the story of my sister, who died before I was born.

"On the Yellow Sea," my mother said, "between Japan and China. We had gone to Japan for the summer, to the mountains behind Nagasaki. It was before we found Kuling, in the Lu mountains of Kiangsi, here in China. It was so hot in the Yangtze Valley that I was afraid for the two children. We had a lovely summer in Japan—the air was cool and healthy up on those mountains. I wanted to stay until October, but your father said he had to be back in September. I shouldn't have listened to him, but I always did. We came back on a Japanese steamship—the *Hiroshima Maru*—and the baby fell ill. I don't know what it was—a high fever and a dysentery. She was only six months old and not strong. And I am always so seasick—I couldn't even hold her. Your father tried to take care of me. And so old Dr. Martin walked up and down the deck with the baby in his arms. I'll never forget how he looked—so tall and straight and the little baby in his arms."

Here her eyes always filled with tears and I always wept

because she did and crept to her side. She held out her hand to me and I clasped it in both mine.

"Then what?" I begged.

"Well, you know, dear. She died in his arms. I was lying in a steamer chair so sick! It was a breathlessly hot night, and there was an old moon, sinking into the sea. And suddenly I saw him stop and look down into the baby's face. And I—knew."

I felt her hand against my cheek, and I longed to comfort her and did comfort her, I suppose, in my childish way. For the story usually ended by her wiping her eyes and saying briskly, "Now let's have a little music before we go to bed," or perhaps she suggested an orange or a mango or a piece of pomelo.

What a volatile thing is memory! When I thought of pomelo, I remembered the delight of that sweet and juicy fruit, a relative of grapefruit but infinitely better in every way, the skin easily detached, the sections free from one another and the flavor superb. In comparison, grapefruit is a little bag of sour water and yielding that only grudgingly. I determined to find pomelo again in Japan, for I had never seen it in my own country.

From my mother's lips, then, I first heard the names of Japanese cities, and saw in my mind's eye, the scenes of mountain and seashore. And my little dead sister was buried in the Christian cemetery in Shanghai, as I knew, for I saw her name with the three others of our family's children, later to be born in China, and to die there, and this before I myself was born in my grandfather's colonial home in West Virginia.

I was nine years old when I first saw Japan for myself, and it was on my first visit to my own country. Our ship stopped at Nagasaki, a Canadian liner, for my father was convinced that only the English really knew how to make a ship and sail it and only an English captain could be trusted to control his crew properly. The city of Nagasaki is a seaport and in those days a small one, a cluster of houses clinging to the shore and pushed close by the high mountains behind. The people there speak a dialect and my father would not let me learn even a few words of it because, he said, it was not a pure Japanese and it was important that the very first words in any foreign language be learned with a perfect accent. He was himself an accomplished linguist and I always obeyed him. It would not have occurred to me to do otherwise. As for the name of Hiroshima, it remained for me the name of the Japanese ship upon which my baby sister died until years later, decades later, when it became the city of the dead, after the bomb fell.

The lobby of the Imperial Hotel is the place where anyone meets anyone from anywhere in the world. I descended there the next morning in an elevator whose operator was a beautiful Japanese girl in kimono. When I walked into the lobby I was approached by a pleasant-faced American woman.

"You look familiar to me," she said. "I am from Ohio. Do I know your name?"

I smiled and shook my head. She smiled and went on. The next instant my hands were caught in a warm grasp, and there before me was an old friend from India.

"Fancy seeing you here," he shouted. "Why aren't you in New Delhi? Our guest room there is waiting for you."

We sat down and exchanged promises and he told me the news of his family, his pretty young wife, much younger than he and married to him against her family's wish, because he is old enough to be her father. But she is a determined young woman and they have been happy together and, to his immense pride, she has given him two sons. He took their pictures from his wallet as he told me about them, and I saw the family standing in their beautiful tropical garden. Ismaya was lovely in her sari, a composed and well-organized young woman, her two little boys clinging to her hands and my friend behind them, tall and handsome and white-haired.

"I look like their grandfather, do I not," he said proudly, "but let me tell you, nevertheless, I advise parents to have children when they are old. My house will never be empty.

I shall leave it before my children do, and when I am gone they will comfort their mother."

My Japanese secretary was at my elbow. She bowed, smiled placatingly and reminded me.

"Please, now is time for press conference. Everybody waiting."

Press conference! In Japan this is a formal and even formidable event, and so it proved for us. The day was hot, May in Tokyo is always hot. We gathered in a large room where a long table stretched across one end. Behind the table chairs were arranged in a row, and we took our places, not hit and miss, but in carefully arranged protocol. First we discussed who was to sit at the table. Then we discussed how we were to sit.

I have been in many press conferences, but there was a peculiar excitement about this one. The big room was crowded with reporters from all papers and magazines—more than seventy. Photographers were numerous but they stood quietly waiting, their cameras poised.

As usual in Japan, the press conference began with speeches from selected persons. In our case, it had been agreed that I was to make a few brief remarks as introduction. What I said was simply that I was happy to be in Japan again, grateful to them for their kindness on my last visit and ready to report progress on our project, *The Big Wave*, a story of Japan. I said that we were pleased to be able to tell them that one of their own companies was co-producing with us, and that I had asked the head of that company to make the formal announcement.

While this was going on the usual pretty girls were serving us glasses of cold tea. A great innovation, this cold tea, influence of the West, certainly, for I did not remember anything but hot tea in earlier days. In the humid heat the cold tea was a blessing. The press sat by submissively without tea, listening closely. Questions are not allowed until speeches are over.

The speech in this case was a notable one. The film executive was well-known and highly respected. He was a man on the young side of middle age, of a calm disposition, complete assurance, and pleasant warmth. I do not understand Japanese, but the speech went on at some length. I wondered what he was saying, for he is usually a man of few words. Our translator told us afterward and privately what had been said. How could I keep from being moved? It was a beautiful speech in which he said that his company felt honored to be part of the picture *The Big Wave*. He said that once he himself had thought, some years ago, of making the book into a picture for he read it at a time of deep depression of mind, when Japan stood before the world for the first time in her proud history a defeated nation. He himself did not know how to recover his own spirits. One day he found this little book and he read it. He felt the author wished to convey through it a communication of hope to the Japanese people, a belief that as they had lived through centuries with the constant possibility of destruction through tidal waves and earthquake, and indeed had often suffered tragically from such natural catastrophes, only to survive each with renewed courage and strength, so again they would survive even defeat. Now, through peculiar coincidence, he had the opportunity in taking part, on behalf of his company, in the making of the film version of the story. Therefore he announced at this press conference that his company had joined the Americans as co-producers of *The Big Wave*.

I listened with gratitude to life. It is the highest reward when a writer hears that a book, written in doubt and solitude, has reached a human heart with a deeper meaning than even the writer had been aware of, as she wrote. It is the something extra, the unexpected return. Many questions followed the speech. They related to production, where the location was, who were to be the actors, and so on. We were not ready yet to announce the actors, for we had many candidates to hear and to see. Negotiations had been going on for weeks with certain stars, and only one was decided upon. We were resolute, we tried to be good-humored in parrying all efforts to extract information about the cast. Suddenly, as we were about to disperse, word came in that negotiations had been successful in regard to one star. We could announce that the well-known Japanese actor, Sessue Hayakawa, would take the role of Old Gentleman in *The Big Wave.*

Upon this the press departed, except for an English reporter, who had not understood Japanese. I spent a few minutes with her, and with one or two other ones who had some special request.

Then everyone was gone and I was alone again. This was the changeless pattern of my days since he had ceased to be himself—a crowd of people, and then no one. I missed him now and especially because he would have enjoyed this press conference. He had presided over many press conferences for me, in many parts of the world, the first one when I came from China, shy and frightened enough to determine in my secret mind that whatever lay ahead, I would not allow my life to be changed. It was changed, of course, the moment he met me in Montreal. I had come by sea and train from Shanghai and although I knew him somewhat through his letters—he wrote the most charming and articulate letters I had ever read—I saw him for the first time, sun-browned and with eyes of a startling blue. I was speechless with my habitual shyness but he was completely at ease, which he always was, everywhere and with anyone, a happy attribute for me, when the next day I faced the formidable press in New York. He knew the reporters, however, and they knew him, for he had begun his professional life as a newspaperman, and they liked him. He set us all at ease, and I found myself answering their questions frankly. Too frankly, he told me afterward with amusement, for when I was asked my age it did not occur to me not to tell it, since in China every year was considered an added honor.

His natural ease made him an excellent chairman, and he was the chairman of an amazing variety of organizations. How often have I not sat in such gatherings and watched him while he, seemingly without effort, allowed every dissident voice to speak, every argument to be heard, and then quietly and in a few words gathered the consensus of opinion into a lucid resolution! He had the rare gift of creating order out of disorder, an editorial gift. But beyond that he had the gift of human understanding which enabled him to select the essential from the nonessential and find points of agreement among those who disagreed.

The little secretary was at my elbow again.

"We have time to go to the old Meiji shrine before you must go to the office and I want you to see it, please, first," she told me. "Tokyo is too new, because of bombing, but Meiji shrine is old and you will feel better to see it."

She summoned a cab and we were whisked through the city, so changed that I would not have known it, new and busy and not beautiful. The palace, however, remained as it was, untouched, and I saw its curved roofs rising, as of old, behind the moated stone walls. Then we entered the Meiji shrine and into the ancient peace. I wandered about the paths, Sumiko tactfully quiet at my side, and came to rest beside the lake. It is as it was when I was a child standing there with my Japanese nurse. The same fat carp, enormous in size, moved lazily among the water lilies, and I told Sumiko this.

"Not the same, please," she said in reply. "In the war many hungry people coming here by night to catch carp and eat them."

I maintained however that some of them were the same. Otherwise even in many years they could not have grown so big.

"Perhaps," she said politely. "Anyhow it is time we will be going, office waiting, doubtless."

We walked to the gate and entered another breakneck taxicab and were whirled to the offices of the big Japanese motion picture company.

Here I pause for a brief interlude.

The most astonishing aspect of new Japan is the Japanese woman. My first Japanese friend was the wife of an Englishman, who lived in a big house on the mountainside near my childhood home in China. I must have known other Japanese women in our goings to and comings from Japan, but none made as deep an impression upon my memory as the lady in the Englishman's house, and this, I think, because I saw her only as she passed by in her sedan chair, borne by four uniformed bearers. She wore kimono always, and her hair was brushed in the high lacquered coiffeur of the ladies of ancient Japan. Her face was powdered white, and her onyx eyes gazed blankly ahead of her until she saw me standing in the dust of the road. In summer she held a small parasol, white silk painted with cherry blossoms, and in winter she wore a brocaded coat over her kimono. We exchanged looks, hers sad and incurious until she smiled at me, and mine wide with wonder and admiration because she was beautiful. A beautiful woman, a handsome man, a pretty child, are sources of joy, merely for the eyes, if for nothing else. It was as this that I remembered her, and because of the smile, somehow as my friend.

In later years I knew more intimately as friend an occasional Japanese woman. She seemed, whoever she was, always remote, somewhat sad, overburdened with duty, and this was true whether she was the wife of a farmer, or of a man of wealth and position. One had always to cross a barrier, disappointment with life, it might be, if not a personal sorrow, before one could reach the inner woman. Perhaps she was never to be reached. Her voice soft and gentle, her demeanor modest and considerate of others, she wore silence as a garment and unless addressed directly she seemed to merge herself with the background.

None of this is true now. The old-fashioned woman, or so it seems to me, has simply disappeared from Japan. Men are very little changed either in appearance or behavior. But women? I cannot describe in one day or one place the extraordinary differences I found in Japanese women. Let me approach the subject gradually, through the individual women I came to know while we made the picture.

Therefore we had no sooner stepped into the offices of the big Japanese motion picture company than I was astounded by what I saw. In other years I would have been greeted by a young man, secretary and assistant to those above. The office would have been staffed by young men. Now, however, it was staffed by young women, all in smart western clothes, and several of them speaking good English. I had the impression, too, that all of them were efficient and pretty. One of them came forward when we appeared and she was certainly very pretty. Her hair was cut short and curled—and let me say here and now, and say again and again, probably, how I deplore the permanent wave in Japan. The smooth straight black hair which was once the glory of Japanese women is now usually cut short and tortured into tightly curled wiglike shapes. Worst of all, it is fashionable, especially for actresses as I was to discover, to dye the black hair a rusty brown. The natural sheen is lost and the muddy color dulls the light cream of the complexion, once so beautiful. Somehow that rusty brown makes the dark eyes ineffective, too, although the Japanese women have the latest in eye make-up and face-powders, liquid or dry or paste.

These modern looks are nothing, however, compared to the modern behavior. Gone is the modest downcast gaze, gone the delicate reserve, gone the indirect approach to men. Instead bold looks, frank speech, a frankly sexual attack on any available man, with preference for the too susceptible American, is the rule of the day.

I am getting ahead of my story. I did not learn all this at once when I entered the offices of the big Japanese film company. What I saw was a bevy of pretty women, neat, composed, efficient, outgoing and apparently indestructibly young, and one of them led us to the inner office. I confess that it was reassuring to see my special friend sitting behind a very modern desk, to be sure, but dressed in a silver gray silk kimono and a pale pink obi. She rose to meet us, bowing deeply with all the old-fashioned grace. Her English is perfect, and I knew she spoke French and German and Italian as well, for part of her work is travel in European countries for Japanese films. There is really nothing old-fashioned about her except her dress. She has a full partnership with her husband and two other associates, both men, in the business. They defer to her wisdom and efficiency and judgment, although I did hear occasional subterranean grumbles from the production manager, to the effect that she was "getting very high these days." Since he was a bachelor, however, in itself reprehensible in Japan for a man over fifty, I did not take him seriously.

The office was a handsome one, modern to the last chair, but a fine old painting hung on the wall and some excellent calligraphy. My friend invited us to be seated, and two or three of the pretty young women brought green tea in Japanese bowls. We sipped and made small talk. She invited me to come and spend a weekend at her country home in Kamakura. I accepted, and of that I shall tell more later. We did not stay long, for it is never good manners in Japan to stay too long on a first call. In fifteen minutes or so, the pretty young woman directed us to the office of the head of the company, a handsome tall man, neither young nor old.

He sat behind his desk and when we entered he rose, bowed and invited us to be seated around a wide long table. He did not speak much English, and his secretary, another pretty young woman, translated for him and for us. He was an intelligent man, as one could see from his fine cultivated face, and a man of the world, assured, self-confident, courteous. The room, as are most offices and business rooms in Japan, was well-designed and sparely but excellently furnished with modern furniture, calm in atmosphere. We sat down at the table in comfortable leather chairs and another pretty girl or two brought us fresh tea. While the men talked through the pretty girl interpreter, I examined the room. On the wall near us, at the end of the room, hung three impressive oil portraits, founders of the company, I was told. These were the only pictures except that, on the opposite walls, as I next observed, there hung a large calendar, whereon was imprinted in poster style the lively form of a bathing beauty in full color, an engaging object upon which the eyes of the three solemn gentlemen, though deceased, still seemed to be fixed. I wondered, laughing inwardly, if one of the neat and pretty girls had hung her counterpart there with humorous intent.

Meanwhile the conversation was proceeding briskly. It was obvious that our host understood English perfectly, but the pretty girl interpreted for him just the same, and with a lively dignity. He obviously relied on her good sense as well as on her competence. What does the Japanese man think of this new woman? I made up my mind to find out somehow, some day. As for her, she appeared to be extremely useful as well as ornamental and, above all, she seemed to be happy. Her ancient sadness was gone. Tragedy had left her, and if what had taken its place was not exactly comedy, it was something vivacious and delightful.

In an amazingly short time the details of our co-operation were fixed—if anything can be said to be fixed in the fluidities and exigencies of film making. The amenities, at least, over, this head of a great triangular company invited us to meet with the remaining third, the production manager. We knew then that we had reached the ultimate, the practical, the man with whom we must deal again and again. To meet him, however, would not be possible until after the weekend, for it was the end of the day, and the day the last of the working week. The weekend in Japanese society has become as important an event as in the most Western country. Nothing could be done until it was over. It was the ideal time to accept the invitation from my friend.

Not far from the huge and modern city of Tokyo is the quiet town of Kamakura. It is famous in Japanese history but famous now because it is the home of some of Japan's best-known writers. My friend's husband was in Europe but she herself came for me in her comfortable and chauffeured car. We drove through the crowded city and the spreading suburbs into the country. It was a sunny afternoon in August, but we did not know it was sunny until we got out of the city because of the smog, which is the same anywhere, and in Tokyo it can be rich and thick, and was that day.

I greatly enjoyed the drive, nevertheless, not only because it gave me the opportunity to see the general outlines of the amazing new Tokyo, at least in one direction, but also because I found that I could really talk with the equally amazing new Japanese woman at my side. She remained beautifully Japanese in her gray silk kimono, her hair smooth, her face amiable and composed, but her mind was cosmopolitan and sophisticated in the true sense of the word. She could and did remain herself anywhere in the world, at ease in any capital. I am accustomed to cosmopolitan and sophisticated women in many countries, but my friend has an unusual and individual quality. One could never mistake her for any but a Japanese, and yet this national saturation of birth and education is only the medium through which she communicates a universal experience and with wisdom and charm. A rose is a rose anywhere in the world, and yet in a Japanese room, arranged in a Japanese vase in a Japanese tokonoma, the rose becomes somehow Japanese. That is my friend.

I asked hundreds of questions, I fear, and was delighted by her frank and informed replies. Two hours slipped past like minutes.

"I have invited some of our writers to meet you," she told me at last. "We will have dinner at a famous inn."

When we arrived at Kamakura, the sun had already set and we went directly to the inn. The car stopped at some distance away, however, and we walked along a narrow footpath, far from the main street of Kamakura. At the end of the path we entered a wooden gate and stepping stones led us from there across a garden to a wide lawn, lit by stone lanterns. The low roofs of the buildings nestled beneath great trees, climbing the abrupt slopes of a mountain behind the inn.

We were late and the guests were waiting for us, a few of Japan's best-loved writers. They all wore dark Japanese kimono, and they sat on a long stone bench, sipping tea. I was introduced to them, one by one, and recognized especially Mr. Kawabata and Jiro Osaragi. Mr. Kawabata is president of the P.E.N. Club of Japan, and had just returned, on the same jet with me, from a visit to North and South America. Since I had never met him, I did not know who he was. He sat just across the aisle from me and I had kept looking at him from time to time.

"That is certainly a great man of Japan," I murmured to my seat mate.

He was not tall and his bones were delicately fine. The eyes, however, revealed the man. They were large, dark, and so lit with intelligence that they were indeed windows through which one looked into a sensitive and brilliant mind.

Now I was looking through them again and with instant recognition.

"It was you—on the jet!" I cried.

He smiled. "I knew you but you didn't know me."

"I know you now," I declared. "I have read your books. I know you went to South America. And—forgive me—I knew when I looked at you that day that you were—somebody."

He laughed at my stupidity, and I admired in my heart his delicately carved features, the firm ivory skin, and the shock of gray hair. He is sixty-two years old and his heavy silk kimono completed his air of an aristocrat. Yet he is also very lively and modern. When I commended, later in the evening, the excellent service on the Japan Airlines he looked mischievous and wagged his head.

"But," he said, "I have a complaint. The hostesses I do not always find very pretty!"

We laughed and my friend explained amicably that this famous writer attracts young girls and therefore is a connoisseur.

We sat for an hour, admiring the moon and enjoying cool fruit juice. The conversation was in English or in Japanese translated for my benefit. Most of the writers did not speak English. Then we were summoned, and we sauntered into the restaurant, took off our shoes at the entrance and walked into a large room, open on two sides to the garden. There to the breeze of a big electric fan, we talked or rested now and then in peaceful silence. I sat beside Jiro Osaragi and my friend translated for us. I had just finished reading for the second time his tender novel, *Homecoming*, a book almost feminine in its grace and subtlety. It was difficult to imagine it written by this tall strong handsome man in middle age. Certainly he was not in the least feminine. But the combination of delicacy and strength, of tenderness and cruelty, is usual in the work of Japanese writers, and is perhaps inherent in Japanese nature.

While we talked, one dish after another was served. It was the season of sea trout, the first good season in a long time, I was told, for sea trout have been destroyed in recent years in some fashion not clear to me, perhaps by atomic waters. At any rate, it was evidently a delicacy now. The trout were served individually roasted on hot stones instead of on plates, each fish placed as though it were swimming on the ocean bed. A line of salt symbolized the beach, a bit of cedar twig the seaweed. It was too exquisite to eat, but we ate and found it delicious. When it was taken away, there came next a length of green bamboo, split, and steamed inside was the tender flesh of young quail. And so on until the end of the meal and we went back to the garden again. There in an open mat shed we had "genghis khan," a Mongol dish of thin sliced beef and vegetables broiled on a charcoal brazier, the forerunner, I daresay, of modern sukiyaki. Properly it should be prepared and eaten outdoors, as we did, in memory of nomad Mongol life. But let me not go into this matter of delicacies, for there is no end to the ingenuity and imagination of the Japanese in culinary matters. The evening passed, too soon the hour of separation arrived. We said our farewells and went our way.

My friend's house is a large one, a combination of ancient and modern Japanese architecture, set in a huge garden and surrounded by a stone wall. As we entered I caught a glimpse of a big living room furnished with western chairs and couches and next to it a room in the Japanese manner. It was too late to linger, however, and I was taken to an upstairs room where a mattress and spotless sheet and pillow were laid on tatami on the floor. She showed me the private bath, felt of a thermos teapot to see if it were hot, and bade me a kind good night.

When we had parted I slid back the shoji and found beyond it a wide veranda overlooking the beautiful garden, just now drenched in golden light from the moon, a light so brilliant that it dimmed the lamps in the stone lanterns. The scene was one of ineffable and eternal peace, the moon riding high over the treetops as it had for unnumbered years. God send that we may watch it ride the same path across the sky for centuries ahead! And yet I was reminded that it was the same moon which only recently had all but led our world to final catastrophe. A great radar, set to catch the slightest unusual outburst of energy anywhere in the world, reported one night that such an outburst was taking place. Alerts flew around the globe. Distance is no problem to transmission, and in two seconds retaliation orders could have been sent and received. Just in time there came a frantic message for delay. What had happened? The full moon had risen and somewhere a bemused young man had neglected to record its rise and thus explain the outburst of energy. Just in time the orders were not sent and the human race was saved.

I turned from the moon and went to bed. The ancient lanterns burned in the gardens all night and the crickets sang while I slept.

In the morning my friend declared that I must see the famous Kamakura shrine. We left the house after a late breakfast and were driven to this ancient shrine, built in the period of the Meiji, some hundred and fifty years ago. It was Sunday and a crowd of sightseers was already there. Young Japan sauntered about, boy and girl, hand in hand, to my astonishment—shades of old Japan!—or side by side, with lunch baskets. Country folk had come into town and the elders walked sedately, here woman still a few paces behind man.

When we approached the great entrance pavilion of fine cedar wood, however, we found a commotion. A television film was in the process of being made. Men dressed in the ancient garb of shogun and daimyo were fencing and fighting in an historical play. We joined the watching crowd. Just as the director, a harried young man wearing dark glasses in the best Hollywood style, had shouted "Action!"—just as the cameras were about to click—action stopped. Into the medieval scene a youth on a bicycle came wheeling down the hill from the shrine. There were loud yells from the director, frantic also in the best Hollywood style, as he warned the young cyclist to take to the woods. The boy obeyed in alarm, and the warriors took their places again and plunged into battle. Alas, at this moment a horde of school children burst into view. Yells again, the children were pushed into the woods, and once more we returned to the past. So it went. There was something symbolic about it, old and new, and one felt the combination everywhere in Japan—new wine in old bottles.

The big living room in that beautiful Japanese house, furnished in western style, is for the family, I discovered when we returned. The Japanese living room was for my friend's mother, now eighty years old. She sat on the floor upon a cushion, her legs folded flat beneath her. Upon a low table before her were her precious possessions, her books, a vase of flowers, her little green parrot in a cage. She could herself have stepped out of centuries past. Yet she was entirely happy in the comfortable modern Japanese home. She was in the family, the center of it, welcome and warm, but she herself was old Japan. Something old and something new again!

The day spent itself in pleasant peace, in conversation and explanation of the garden and library. I rode back to Tokyo alone in the evening in the comfortable, air-conditioned, made-in-Japan car and reflected upon the weekend. One small incident stayed above all others in my mind. In the quiet luxurious house there was a younger sister, gentle and unobtrusive and no longer young. I had refrained from asking questions about her. It was none of my business why she was there. She was helpful, she was content. But my inveterate, uncontrollable, insatiable novelist's curiosity got the better of me just before I left. I really am on terms of good friendship with this Japanese family, but I felt compelled to begin with an apology.

"I am ashamed to ask so many questions," I told my friend. "Yet if I do not ask, how shall I know?"

"Ask whatever you like," she told me kindly.

I asked, "Please, has your younger sister never married? It is so unusual."

There was an instant's hesitation on that calm older sister's face. Then she answered. "She did marry once, twenty years ago. He was a good man—an old friend . . . Four days after the wedding she came home."

I waited and hoped that I would not ask another question. But no, it came rushing to my lips. "Why did she come home?"

The elder sister answered quite simply. "We don't know. We have never liked to ask."

I asked no more questions. Twenty years and they do not like to ask! The answer revealed the exquisite reticence of an entire people . . . No, not new wine in old bottles. Reverse the metaphor—old wine in new bottles. The difference is subtle but profound.

The next morning we met by appointment the production manager. He is an important figure in any film company, but in that Japanese company he held the position of prime minister. Everything was referred to him, miracles were expected, and all yeas and nays from the top came through him.

On Monday morning, then, very hot, we were ushered into his office by a pretty girl. We beheld a huge Japanese man in shirt sleeves with wild hair, wild eyes, heavy jowls, a pursed mouth, a loud voice. He was bellowing into one telephone while three other telephones in various parts of the room were occupied by three pretty girls, each speaking from his dictation but in soft pretty voices. He rolled his huge fiery eyes at us but did not acknowledge us otherwise, except by an imperious wave of his enormous hand bidding us to be seated. We sat down in low chairs around a low table and a pretty girl served tea while we waited. He broke off the conversation at last with a fierce bellow and came to greet us, all cordiality and kindness and impatience and a certain air of desperation, which later we learned was his habitual mood.

He put aside formalities and spoke with apparent frankness—certainly frankness of the moment. I make this qualification, for I have learned even in my own country that the charming and disarming frankness of the permanent citizens of the theater world does not necessarily convey what is commonly called truth. Truth in the theater may be strictly momentary and confined within the limits of hope, expectation, or even possibly, intention. The production manager therefore belonged strictly to the theater world. He spoke in Japanese, his interpreter one of the pretty young women educated in the United States, who softened what he said without destroying its force. She was very skillful. But we did not yet really know him. That day he merely said, looking harassed, that he would do everything he could to help us, asking us only one favor. We were to allow him to arrange financial matters with the cast. Japanese film companies, he told us, were not very favorable to co-producing American pictures. Americans paid absurd salaries and made actors discontented and unruly afterward when dealing with their own Japanese companies. He banged his big fist on the table. Witness, he roared, what had happened in Italy! It must not happen in Japan! We promised, and took our leave.

Now that we had met all the important persons, programing was the next task. In making a motion picture film, programing is as important as the assembling of input material for a computing machine. All the necessary ingredients must be provided at once and in such order that the proper result is assured. Thus we had not only to consider the arrangements with our co-operating Japanese film company, but we had at the same time to think of finding locations for the filming as well as choosing actors and composer and cameraman and all the et ceteras that go into the vast complexity of a film. Now that our picture is finished, I find that I have a great deal more respect for all motion pictures, even the bad ones, than I had before. However unsatisfactory they may be from the artistic viewpoint, immense pain and effort, many disappointments and much agony went into their making, not to mention weariness of mind and body. To make a film is big business.

While the production manager was fulfilling his promises about helping us to find our cast, we decided to set to work on locations. Seacoast, fisherman's house, farmhouse, a gentleman's home and a live volcano were the sets we needed. Landscape and incident would enrich the story that was to be lived in these sets. There was also to be the tidal wave but more of that later.

We went into consultation as to what we should do first, now that preliminary contacts had been made, and we decided upon finding locations and especially the volcano. We hoped to find everything near Tokyo if possible, for the studios are in Tokyo. Privately I had no such hope, for in my memory I saw a little village set in a wide cove beside the sea, the terraced hillside of a farm above it, and somewhere near it Old Gentleman's house. Such a landscape was not, I was sure, to be found near Tokyo. The volcano, however, was another matter. The strange black island of Oshima is not far away from that city—only a few hours by shaky little coastal steamer, and forty-five minutes by air. We decided on the ship, still hoping that as we sailed along the indented shores we might discover a fishing village to which we could return. The ocean was likely to be rough, as we were told, and certainly the ship was small. It was a clean little ship, however, and when we went aboard it was already filled with touring school children and their teachers.

School children are the darlings of Japan, as anyone can see. They are all dressed in western clothes nowadays and from the smallest village and the most ancient, one sees at eight o'clock in the morning bevies of smartly dressed little boys and girls, all spotlessly clean, each with a knapsack and a thermos, wending their way to school. On holidays or special days they proceed in the same spotless state to various famous places, always in order and apparently very happy.

On the little steamer that day the crowd of school children was appallingly large, and the ship sank far below the waterline. No one seemed afraid, however, and since the day was fine and the sea bright with whitecaps, I decided to cast fear aside and enjoy the brief voyage. We skirted the superbly beautiful coastline all morning without seeing a village that looked possible, and drew up at last at a wide dock and found ourselves in the port. We were to spend the night and return in the morning ship, and we went at once to the hotel. It was a large place, a summer hotel, a little on the shabby side as most summer hotels are inclined to be anywhere, and I found to my embarrassment that I had been assigned to the Emperor's suite. The cordial innkeeper assured me that the Emperor and Empress had occupied it only the week before and had found it so comfortable that they had not wanted to get up for breakfast, which put me in such awe that I begged for a less exalted room. We then engaged a car and were driven around the island and to the volcano.

Oshima is black. I thought of the song that King Solomon sang to his dark love. "Thou art dark, but comely." So it is with Oshima. The entire island is the overflow of the volcano, and this means that the soil is lava, crushed by time and weather. There are no farms but the valleys and lower hillsides are green with wild camellias. When they are in bloom in early spring the island is transformed into a bower, famous in all Japan. The livelihood of the people depends, however, not upon the flowers but upon the oil extracted from their seed pods. Camellia oil—how luxurious it sounds! Actually it is a thin liquid, as clear as water and as scentless. It is used for everything from cookery to hair oil.

A few fishing villages cling to the coast of the island and the population is small because of the poverty of the land. The coastline is wild and I stopped the car often so that I might enjoy the fearful beauty of high white surf crashing against the ebony-black cliffs.

The roads were rough and we were glad to give up our search at last and go to the volcano itself. All day I had seen it smoking and steaming above us and rolling out its clouds of sulphur-yellow gas, an awesome sight. When we reached its base we were really appalled. The mountains were smooth and black and completely devoid of grass or even of camellia trees. Smoke and gas and steam had killed everything for hundreds of square miles and the gaunt mountains encircling the volcano raised their black crests against the sky. So may the moon look when the first astronaut descends and like an astronaut I felt, so incredible did it seem that this could be our Earth. Nor could we approach the crater, not at least upon this journey. The winding road, I was told, was seven to ten miles long, and one must ride horseback. Scores of horses stood saddled and waiting with their eager owners. It was not necessary for us, however, to climb the volcano to know that we had found what we were looking for. I stood for a long time on top of a bare black hill at the foot of the volcano and saw the setting sun redden the swirling white steam until it looked like flames of living fire. Here we would come later with our actors and cameramen and crew. We would climb to the top of the crater and take the scene of our little hero, Yukio, the farmer's son, as he stands looking down into the center of our globe.

And shall I ever forget, before we returned to Tokyo, we saw unexpectedly, that afternoon, the snowy cone of Mount Fuji, rising above the clouds and halfway up the sky. Visitors in Japan may stay for months and not see Fuji. It is entirely by chance and the grace of God whether the sacred mountain appears before human eyes. We were driving on a hillside road in the middle of the afternoon, the sky was turbulent with clouds, and while I dreamed of the vision I dared not hope. Suddenly I saw it, the perfect crest, white against a field of sudden blue sky. A few, a very few, famous sights are better than the rumor of their beauty. The Taj Mahal is one of these and Fuji is another. We stopped for three and a half minutes to gaze in delight and awe. Then clouds hid again the majestic shape.

I opened my eyes in Tokyo the next morning at five o'clock, widely awake, totally aware. I had been summoned in some way, not by a voice or at least I did not hear a voice. I was simply conscious somehow of having been summoned. The room was neither dark nor light. Night had ended but dawn was not yet come. I lay motionless in my bed, listening, waiting, convinced that someone was trying to reach me. Slowly the impression faded away and I was alone again, yet not as before. There was still something to come. I must be ready for it.

At quarter to six o'clock the telephone rang. I knew immediately what the message would be.

"Overseas call, please," a voice said. "From the United States, please, Pennsylvania calling—are you ready?"

"I am waiting for it," I said. I knew now that I had been waiting for an hour.

"Stand by, please," the voice said.

I had been standing by for an hour and I continued. In seven minutes, my watch on the table under my eyes, my daughter's voice came to me over the thousands of miles of land and sea between us.

"Mother?"

"Yes, darling."

"I have to tell you something. Are you ready?"

"Yes, darling."

"Mother." The clear brave young voice faltered and went on resolutely. "Mother, Dad left us this morning in his sleep."

"I thought that was what you had to tell me."

"How did you know?"

"I just—knew."

"Will you come home?"

"Today—on the first jet."

"We'll meet you in New York."

"I'll cable as soon as I know the flight."

"Everybody has come home. We're all here. We'll take care of everything until you come."

"I know."

We exchanged the few private words, heart spoke to heart, and I hung up. For a moment there was the longing, oh, that I had never left, oh, that I could have been there when he went. I put it aside. I had discussed this very moment thoroughly with our family physician. Years ago he had said in answer to my question, "It may be many years away, it may be tomorrow. You must continue to live exactly as you have. His heart is strong, his digestion is perfect—I think he will live a long time. But remember, whenever it comes, however it comes, you can have done nothing to prevent it. Even I could not, though I might be sitting at his side."

He had hesitated, then continued. "The brain is severely damaged. Of course you must expect a total change in personality—we don't know—"

That brilliant brain, responding so quickly to my every thought—yes, there had been a change in personality. The man I knew so well, the wise companion, became someone else, a trusting child, a gentle helpless infant, whom no one could help loving. We were fortunate, even so. When the brain fails and only the body is left, it is true that there is sometimes a terrifying change in the personality. The Chinese believe the human being has three souls and seven earthly spirits. When the souls depart, only the earthly spirits are left, the person becomes evil and cruel in unpredictable ways. It was not so with him. His earthly spirits were all of a piece with his three souls. He continued what he had always been: lovable, patient, unwilling to cause trouble, as always, except that slowly there ceased to be communication. Language was lost, eyesight failed, the brain ceased to live except in sleep.

It was too early to wake anyone with the news and there was no one, in any case, who could have shared my thoughts or my memories. How quickly, in one instant, years of happy life become only memories! The long slow preparation of the past seven years was now complete. The day I had dreaded had come. The final loneliness was here.

There was no concealing the news. Someone in the telephone office told someone else. Within an hour the telephone was ringing and friends were at my door. None of it seemed near or real. I heard their voices asking. I heard my own replies. Yes, it is true and I must get the first jet home. No seats were available but again friends managed to get one for me. Someone gave up his place when he heard. But the first jet was to leave at midnight and I had the whole day to live through somehow. The kindness, the rising sympathy, became too much to bear. I knew that I must get out of the city, into the country, away from telephones, and where no one could knock on my door.

At that moment Miki said, "Come to my house for the day."

Miki, my friend, lives about two hours from Tokyo. A good train service takes one there swiftly and in comfort—Japanese trains are excellent—but we went in her car. When we reached the little town near which she lives, we drove straight through to the foot of a steep hill that is not quite a mountain, and the gate opened to admit us.

"From here up you will have to walk," Miki said briskly.

There was comfort in that confident, practical voice, relief in knowing that Miki would conduct herself exactly as though I had merely come to spend an ordinary day. I had never, as a matter of fact, seen her home. She had been to my home in Pennsylvania more than once. I knew about her work for the half-American children born in Japan. She is unique among Japanese women. Why do I say Japanese? She is simply unique. I have never know a woman like her. She is modern to the last cell of her brain, but her blood is ancient and highborn Japanese. She belongs to one of the great families of Japan and her husband has held many honored posts. She has lived in Europe and she visits the United States once or twice a year. She wears western dress because she can move more freely in it, but anywhere in the world she could only be Japanese. She laughs at her own looks and calls herself "pumpkin-face," and it is true her face is round, but she is handsome and her eyes are lively and her air that of a person accustomed to being listened to. Her own story as she tells it herself is something like this:

One day, during the most rigorous period of the war, she entered a train to go to the country and hunt for food. The train was crowded, and she took the last seat. As she sat down a bundle fell into her lap from the baggage rack above her head. It was wrapped in newspaper and the papers were loose. She unwrapped it in order to wrap it again more tightly and there before her horrified eyes was a little new-born baby boy. He was dead. At that moment military police came into the car to search for black marketeers. They saw what she had on her lap and immediately arrested her for trying to dispose of a dead child. They thought the child was hers. She had a bad few minutes until an old farmer spoke up for her.

"It is not her child. A young woman came in and put that bundle up on the rack and went away again."

The police were finally convinced and she was saved. But, as she tells it, she never forgot that little dead baby."I feel the weight of that dead baby on my knees forever," she always says.

Days later, as she was walking in her beautiful garden in the early morning, she noticed something moving under a big bush. It was, she thought, a rabbit. She stooped to see whether it was injured, and discovered a tiny baby. Some desperate young mother had left it there. She drew the child out and took him to the house and cared for him. From then on she has devoted herself to the half-American children born in Japan. What began with a small dead body has grown into a great living work for thousands of children, born of Japanese mothers and fathered by American men, black and white. She has organized an adoption agency of her own and has placed more than a thousand half-American orphans with American parents in the United States. The children are still being born and she is still placing them. But many of them live with her and will continue in her home until they are grown and able to take care of themselves.

On that day as I climbed the hill I heard their voices from above, shouting, laughing, screaming in play. The path, winding among great trees, was paved with stone, and stone steps led up the steepest slopes. The day was beautifully mild and the sunshine fell between the tree trunks upon the moss-covered earth. Far below us the village houses clustered together, their roofs of thatch and tile. I walked slowly, I remember, my usually strong energies sapped from within. I asked questions and heard her answers and all the time I was far away from everyone and near to none. It was as though I were suspended, weightless, in space. Mind and heart were numb, I realized suddenly that she was talking and I did not know what she had said.

"How many children have you here, Miki?" I asked, merely to have something to say.

"One hundred and forty-eight," she told me. She was walking at her habitual brisk speed and she stopped, waiting for me to catch up.

One hundred and forty-eight! They were scattered everywhere in the fine old Japanese buildings and gardens of Miki's ancestral home. She has built some modern houses, too, utilitarian for school and dormitories. In one of the dormitories I saw two little girls absorbed in the care of a rabbit and some field mice. The children were allowed to have their pets near them and each child had a special place for his own private possessions. Most orphanages are sad places but somehow Miki had made her huge establishment a home instead of an orphanage. About half of the children, I noticed, were the children of Negro fathers. The proportion born is, of course, much lower, but most of the half-white children have been adopted, and only a few of the half-Negro ones, for the simple reason that few Negro couples can afford the cost of adoption.

We wandered about the grounds, stopping here and there to look at some special point of interest. Miki's great delight is the school, and she was working hard now for her senior high school building. She had been engaged in a neck-and-neck race for the last ten years on this business of school, keeping just ahead of her children. We looked at all the schoolrooms, I remember, and I noticed on each door a small map in bronze. Upon examination, each map proved to be that of a State in the United States, and Miki answered my question.

"Each year I go to your country and concentrate my appeal on one State. When the people there give me enough money for one more schoolroom I come back and add it to my school building. Then in thanks I put on the door a map of the State and on the map is engraved my appreciation to the people of the State."

"But your maps are so different in relative size from the reality," I said. "Rhode Island, for example, is quite big here, though actually it is our smallest state."

She opened another door while I spoke and I looked into a tiny room, not much larger than a closet and much too small for a schoolroom. A storage space, possibly? On the door was a map no bigger than the palm of my hand. It expressed appreciation to the people of Texas!

Miki laughed at my astonishment. "Texas people like to keep their money for Texas," she said frankly. "I thank them just the same for what they gave me for their half-Texan children, but you see Texas is very small here in our school house."

There was not the slightest resentment in Miki's cheerful voice. It expressed merely an acceptance of people as she finds them. She continued to lead the way amiably through the clean kitchens and the dining rooms. The children took care of themselves to a large degree, and everywhere children were helping, chattering and laughing as they worked. She made a few corrections here and there and the children listened with attention but without fear. When she speaks it is firmly and to the point and she is not sentimental. I thought I observed a secret fondness, however, for what she calls "my naughty boy" or "my naughty girl." It is true that she appreciates, even enjoys, the mischief that expressed itself as often here as anywhere. She explained that she herself had been "a naughty girl" when she was small and now she laughs and at the same time administers the necessary scolding or punishment. She is not afraid of her children and they know she has them all in her heart. She herself sleeps, I discovered, in a room with the naughtiest and the newest.

"Sometimes a naughty boy wants to run away," she told me. "He is used to wild freedom on the streets. When I think he will try to run away, I tie a strong string around his ankle that he cannot untie, and the other string to my own ankle. If he runs in the night I wake and catch him."

Her greatest pride is in her theater and this she kept until the last as a final treat. Miki is an actress born, there is no doubt of it. Whatever she does is dramatic and strong. She admits that she loves the theater above all else. Therefore in the center of the place which is her life, she has created a beautiful little theater, modern and convenient, and here the children present plays and dances.

"After luncheon," she promised, "my children will sing and dance for you."

Yes, the morning which loomed ahead of me in centuries had already passed. The sun had climbed to zenith, and the gong was ringing for the children. They threw down their games and ran to the dining room. I had not once forgotten that I am alone in the world, but somehow the eternal knowledge had not penetrated deeply enough to me. All day Miki had been showing me life, she had made me walk from one center of life to another. And now, before we ourselves went to luncheon, she had one more gift of life for me.

"We will look at the babies," she said.

We walked to the end of the garden and there, in a sunny house built for babies, we saw them, the tiny babies newly born, the little ones learning to sit up and to walk. Kind women were caring for them and the babies clung to them. It comforted me to see how the babies turned away from me, a stranger, to those who cared for them. Too often I have visited orphanages where the children ran to strangers and clung to us when we left.

"They will all go for adoption," Miki said, "except this little one who is mentally retarded. I shall have to think of something for him. . . . This little girl goes to New York. This boy is leaving next week for San Francisco. I am taking them myself—eleven babies to their new American parents. I fly over North Pole."

I looked at each little one closely and with love. They are always beautiful children, these who carry the East and the West in their veins. Kipling forgot about them when he said there could be no meeting of East and West. They have always met, as true hearts must meet, in love if not in politics. It is love that brings human beings together, many kinds of love, but only love. I left the little children with reluctance, for they brought me deep comfort. Love is stronger than hate and life is stronger than death.

We walked back through the gardens now in full sunshine, and came to an enormous Japanese house, built of aged wood, and open along one full side to what had once been a fine Japanese garden but was now a dusty bare baseball field. A group of boys had eaten their food in a hurry and were back on the field with bats and balls. We circled them and entered the house, taking off our shoes on the lowest step. From thence it was only one more step into Miki's beautiful big living room. It has the same cosmopolitan mixture of East and West that Miki herself has. At one end of the room deep satin-covered couches, somewhat worn, made a hospitable circle. Handsome old screens stood at various places and the walls were covered with ancient scrolls and modern photographs. At the far end of the room was a low dining table, long and wide, and two polished antique cabinets.

"I know you like Chinese food," Miki told me as we came in. "So I have therefore invited a Chinese general, my old friend, and best restaurateur in Tokyo, to provide our luncheon."

The General appeared from a distant corner of the room and presented himself, an extremely handsome man, white-haired and looking fit and slim. It is quite usual for Chinese generals, euphemistically retired, to become restaurateurs in the capitals of foreign countries. They are men of taste, but also, perhaps, they have prudently kept with them their own private cooks on the theory that if a man is assured of fine cookery he can endure anything, including defeat in battle. It may even be that the thought of his good cook has helped a general to stop fighting before dinner. Not all generals remain as slim as General Wang, however.

I wish I could convey the exquisite tact of my hostess and of my fellow guests during the delicious Chinese meal. Each of them knew what had happened to me, and yet no one spoke of it. They did not, on the other hand, pretend to a false cheerfulness. They talked with quiet interest of various subjects, skillfully rousing my attention if I sank too long into silence, distracting me by pleasant interchange which demanded response, and urging me to try one delicacy after another, not out of appetite, of which they knew I had none, but as a courtesy to the cook who would be hurt if I did not eat. Once, I remember, I heard a telephone ring but it was to be postponed, apparently, until the meal was over. I do not remember what the dishes were. I cannot recall what the conversation was about. I listened and smiled and made what I think were suitable replies, and was upheld not by what was being said, but by that strong atmosphere of complete understanding never put into words. I do remember that a beautiful Japanese woman, her gray hair in a modern Italian haircut, sat at one end of the table. She wore a satin-soft, red kimono and spoke excellent English. I remember that she said she had just returned from Paris, and that she was Miki's sister-in-law.

I remember, too, that a vigorous baseball game went on while we ate, and I heard again and again the sharp click of bat against ball, the sounds of running feet, screams and clapping hands. In the midst of all this Miki kept a lively eye on the game and every now and again she shouted instructions or approval.

When the meal was over, Miki told me a call had come for me from overseas. She went with me then into a small room and closed the door and handed me the receiver. Across the thousands of miles of earth and sea I heard my daughter's voice again as clearly as though she were in the next room.

"Mother, we have planned everything but we want to know if you approve. The service will be day after tomorrow and our own minister, of course, will take charge. We thought it would be best to have it in the library because he loved that room, you know. He could—the casket could be set in front of the fireplace—and nobody there except the people from the farm and the house—and the nurses who took care of him—and all of us. Then we'll take him to the family cemetery—no flowers, we thought, but asking people to give the money to Welcome House."

The children had planned everything as I would have done and now it remained only for me to get home quickly.

I said yes, yes, yes, over and over again and gave my love and thanks to them all. Then when I had hung up the receiver, it was suddenly all too much. For the first time I let myself feel, and acknowledge, that it had all been too much from that day, seven years ago, in a sunny park in Sheridan, Wyoming, when the first blow had fallen. Such a little blow it had seemed at the time—no more than a mild heat stroke, we thought. We had planned for several years to take a family summer trip through the West, to Yellowstone Park and then into Oregon and Washington. It had been a comfortable and happy time, all of us in a big air-conditioned car, driven by our tried and true chauffeur. "The trip will be good for him," our family doctor had said, "if he does not do the driving."

So it had seemed, until that sunny day. The next day we were to go on to Yellowstone. The next day, instead, he and I stayed in a pleasant ranch house while the children went on and came back and we all went home, still thinking it was nothing, but that we had better go home, at any rate to be near our own doctor. The Sheridan doctor had not been quite sure it was a heat stroke. Later we knew it was not. But he seemed as well as ever, as vigorous, still carrying on his busy life in the New York offices and in the country office at home.

I hid my face with my hands when I put up the receiver and struggled with myself. And Miki, with that delicacy so natural to Asia, ancient and accustomed to human sorrow, sat beside me in silence, not putting forth her hand to touch me, knowing that all comfort was vain, except the comfort of a friend sitting quietly beside me. I struggled through and wiped my eyes and Miki rose.

"The children are waiting for us," she said.

Those were her words, but what she really said was that I must live and begin now to live. Death must not interrupt life. There were others waiting for us. I followed her out of the small room and she led me to the theater.

The audience was the older children, the staff and ourselves. The entertainment was dancing and music, the music a jazz band and folk singing. What interested me was the children. They were strikingly beautiful, without exception, and obviously talented. The girls in kimono did Japanese dances with fans and flowers in the ancient style. The jazz band was made up of boys, many of them half-Negro, and they were handsome indeed.

I confess on that day, when I sat looking at Miki's children and listening to them, it seemed to me that I could never smile again. Yet the children brought me their own comfort and in love and determination I decided that, insofar as I was able, I would help Miki to find families for them.

The afternoon came to an end. It was time to go back to Tokyo and time to go home. Miki refused to leave me until the last moment.

The jet took off at midnight. Friends came to see me off and their kindness and affection wrapped me around. But they had to return to their own lives and I had mine to face, and there was a certain comfort in being at last among strangers, to whom I need make no response. I found my seat, fastened my belt and leaned back and closed my eyes. It was the first moment that I had been totally alone since the moment that morning when the world had changed. Long ago, when I knew my child was to be permanently retarded, I learned that there are two kinds of sorrow, one which can be assuaged and one which cannot be assuaged. This one was different, yet alike in that it, too, was not to be assuaged. Nevertheless, years ago I had learned the technique of acceptance. The first step is simply to yield one's self to the situation. It is a process of the spirit but it begins with body. There, belted into my seat while the aircraft rose into the black sky of night, I consciously yielded my body, muscle by muscle, bone by bone. I ceased to resist, I ceased to struggle. Let come what would, I could do nothing to change what had already happened. The aircraft contained me, controlled me, and isolated me.

In a curious way spirit must sometimes follow body, just

as at other times spirit leads. Now as the body yielded itself to the will, the spirit found it easier also to yield to the same command. Life can be inexorable but death is always inexorable. The next step is to recognize inexorability. The past becomes static. It is history and the facts of history cannot be changed. What has been done is done. One can learn from the past, one can treasure the past, but it cannot be changed. Twenty-five years had been lived in happiness, but they were lived. The End had been written. One does not go on writing a book after those two words have finished it. Another book has to be begun.

It cannot begin at once. There has to be time for total relaxation, total recognition of inexorability, total realization that the life of the past is over. Only then can new strength be summoned. I doubt even that it can be summoned. It has to grow from the very sources of the being into a new will to live. As far as the will could go that night, as the jet darted its way among cloud and stars, it was only to command the body to yield and the spirit to withdraw. At last I slept.

I looked at my watch. It was three o'clock in the morning. Time was meaningless in this swift flight and the sky was already light. I had left Tokyo the night before, Sunday, but I would reach New York on Monday morning, after another day and night of living, if not of time. I was beginning to understand the relativity of time to space and speed. What miracle that Einstein was born in coincidence with the practical experience of jets and rockets in space! My mind, unable as yet to face the profound change in my own life, explored the meaning of eternity, time without beginning and without end. Whatever exists now, has always existed and always will, the universal and eternal law only that of change. And yet change can be frightening. If death is only a change, then what is the change? He knew and I did not. At a moment in his sleep he had died. He was at one instant alive and at the next instant dead. That is, at one instant he had been this, and at the next instant that, the same and yet different.

Where is he now?

Einstein proved to us that mass is interchangeable with energy. This sentence, so simply written, resulted in the awakening of my own mind to the new age. It was more than an awakening of the mind. It was the conversion of my soul, the clarification of my spirit, the unification of my whole being. I had a new conception of death, a new approach to life. Like Saul of Tarsus, I was proceeding on my way when a light broke upon me, a burning illumination that changed my course. This equation, which Einstein crystallized into a few brief symbols, is the key to our universe and doubtless to many more beyond. What was once mass can become energy, is potential energy even while it is mass. Is this the scientific proof of what we call soul?

While the heart bled in private, my mind turned and twisted itself in searching. I reflected upon the miracle of the magic machines, the computors, the thinking mechanism expressed in concrete material. They are built upon the principle of the human brain, but the brain is infinitely more complex, the nodes infinitely more numerous. The brain can create new ideas, the machines cannot, as yet. Nevertheless the principle is the same. We know how to build brains in crude materials, if not in human stuff.

True, there are two schools of thought among the scientists who create the machines. Some believe the machines can be developed into true brains, equal to the human brain and in a few ways even surpassing it. A human brain, for example, would need a lifetime in which to arrive at certain astronomical mathematical conclusions. The machine, given the necessary input, can reach the conclusions in minutes. Other scientists, however, believe that the machine can never duplicate the human brain. There is, they maintain, an element in the human brain, a will, an awareness, a conscience—call it soul, or whatever—which cannot be expressed through the material of a machine.

I hope the second school is nearer the truth. I must believe it is, for if we are only machines, our mass merely flesh instead of metal, then when the mass decays—ah, but wait! Mass cannot be lost, it can only be changed. Changed into what? That is what we must know, will know, some day. And I am encouraged in this faith, for we do know that in this unbelievable universe in which we live, there are no absolutes. Even parallel lines, reaching into infinity, meet somewhere yonder.

Where are you? Do you know I am here high above the earth? Are you here, too? How quickly does the change come? Does the energy you now are transpose itself instantly to some other place? Do you live beyond the barriers of airless space? We are out of communication—

Communication—this is now to be thought of, wondered about, investigated. There is a heavy cordon of deadly radioactivity encircling the earth, the only exits at the two poles. Are those exits for a special purpose? It is incredible that we can no longer communicate. When he was here we often laughed because our thoughts broke into identical words, the same thoughts at the same moment. Yet he was skeptical of any notion of the supernatural. Although he had warm compassion, complete integrity, and unfailing moral conviction, he would not allow the hopes and premises of religion. He insisted on complete independence as a human being.

"We know nothing of the future," he said. "I shan't fool myself or allow myself to be fooled."

"But not knowing doesn't mean there is nothing to be known," I said.

"Whatever there is," he retorted, "I shall know in due course—or not know, because I shall cease to be."

That was the great argument between us, Hamlet's question asked in universal terms. Are we to be or not to be? He said we are not to be. I denied such positive belief. How could we say no, when we did not know that yes was impossible? Now he knows and I do not.

It is rather unfair of you. I thought we would always know together. You might find a way of telling me. Are you or are you not?

I pressed the question into the night and then withdrew

it in a panic. I really do not want to know the truth. If he exists it will make the waiting alone intolerable. And I cannot bear to know that he does not exist. Let me wait until I find out for myself, through experience. If I am right, my first words to him as I step over will be spoken in love and triumph.

"Here I am. Now we know."

Until then I continue as we were before, he doubting, I believing. Yes, I think I still believe, although I have not yet discovered how to know. Faith, the saints have told us through the ages; possibility, the scientists are saying today, because so much we once thought impossible is now possible. Saints and scientists—

The light of dawn that permeates a jet aircraft is wonderfully beautiful. We were flying into the sunrise, into a fountain of light, glorious and majestic, rising over the curved edge of the globe. People woke and stirred and gazed out of the small windows. There was a fragrance of coffee in the air, a spick-and-span hostess was alert and ready with fruit juice. At my side a passenger rose and sauntered down the aisle. I had not been aware of the presence of this stranger all night, and yet I knew he was there. Sooner or later we would speak, but I had sheltered myself in the darkness. Now day had begun, the first day of my new and solitary life. It did not matter how many people surrounded me, within myself would be, from now on, a permanent solitude. What did this mean? What could it mean? It remained to be discovered. I must not insist upon knowing everything at once. Long ago I had learned that if one is to be patient with others, one must also be patient with one's self.

I did not learn this lesson all at once. I was often impatient with myself, and with myself above all others, until I realized, I think through the practice of music, that learning is a day-by-day process. One can work fourteen hours solidly on memorizing a Beethoven sonata for a single performance, but this learning is not permanent. To hold the music forever in one's mental grasp, it must also be absorbed spiritually—that is to say, it must become a part of one's being over a period of time and through continuing practice. What I had to discover about solitude, what I had to learn about its use, its meaning, was only to be acquired through daily life and new experience. Going to the theater alone, for example, had taken effort when he was no longer able to go with me. We loved the theater, he and I, and some of our happiest hours were spent there. To laugh together through a Gilbert and Sullivan evening—well, he loved Gilbert and Sullivan and could play and sing those operettas by the hour, and all our children knew the songs. I had to learn to enjoy them, for they were foreign to me. But we were eclectic and enjoyed theater, whatever it was, indignant only when a play was so obviously tripe that it was a desecration of a noble and ancient art. He would certainly have been disappointed with me, not to say disgusted, if I had given up theater because I must go alone. Flashes of this sort of incidental perception broke irrelevantly into my mind, and I put them off. Day by day was the way I had long ago learned to live and today was here, thousands of feet above the earth, enclosed in this swiftly moving silver shell, surrounded by people I had never seen before and probably never would see again.

There is a comfort at once superficial and organic in the necessities of washing and clothing the body, in eating and drinking. It seemed to me when I faced the mirror that never again would I care about how I looked, since I would never again hear his words of appreciation and praise. I knew of course that I could not trust him for truth on that score. He was too generous, and no one else could possibly see me as he did. I did not for a moment believe I was at all what he said I was. As a woman, nevertheless, I liked to hear even what I knew could not be true and so long as he believed it, what did it matter?

Was this same face the one I had been compelled to look at for so many years? I was another person, and the face must belong to someone else. Nevertheless I washed and made it up as usual and took the habitual care with my long hair. That hair! Even as a little girl it was my bane, always long and soft and tangled. In those days it was honey yellow and my mother would not cut it, and she coaxed me when I cried and praised me when she had combed it out and tied a ribbon about my head. She made curls when I was small and then long braids and I longed for the day when I was grown up and could cut it all off and I did, as soon as I could, and then let it grow again because he wanted it long. Now I could cut it again, since he would never see it, and then knew at the same moment that I never would cut it, although its length was silver instead of gold. Without caring in the least, my hands did their habitual task and I could not believe, when I looked in the mirror, that I looked the same, after all, but I did.

When I returned to my seat, the stewardess gave me breakfast and I could smell the coffee and bacon and toast. Though the spirit was remote and took no part in any of this, the body performed as usual. O cruel flesh!

And everyone in the jet was awake now and I knew no one and no one knew me, for which I was grateful. The stewardess took the breakfast tray away at last, half-finished, and I tried to read a Japanese novel and then put it away. I did not want a love story or even a story of human beings and I opened my dressing case and took from it a thin book, *Science and Human Values*, by J. Bronowski. This book I read all morning, my mind working sharply apart from my individual life.

> Whether our work is art or science or the daily work of society, it is only the form in which we explore our experience which is different; the need to explore remains the same. That is why, at the bottom, the society of scientists is more important than their discoveries. What science has to teach here is not its techniques but its spirit; the irresistible need to explore. . . . For this is the lesson of science, that the concept is more profound than the laws and the act of judging more critical than the judgment. In a book I wrote about poetry I said:

"Poetry does not move us to be just or unjust, in itself. It moves us to thoughts in whose light justice and injustice are seen in fearful sharpness of outline."

What is true of poetry is true of all creative thought. And what I said then of one value is true of all human values. The values by which we are to survive are no rules for just and unjust conduct but are those deeper illuminations in whose light justice and injustice, good and evil, means and ends, are seen in fearful sharpness of outline.

Here the book ended and I closed it, and was grateful for a thinking mind that spoke to mind. How grateful indeed am I to my scholarly parents, those two who from my earliest years taught me by their example to find release and courage and strength in the use of the mind! Whatever the individual sorrow and however absolute the individual solitude, the mind, trained in use and by use, continues to explore. I carried within my skull my own implement. I need not, I must not, retreat or pause or cease to grow because I walk my way alone.

A strange peace, warm and alive, flowed through me. I leaned my head back against the seat and closed my eyes. I remember smiling to myself, though I do not know why. It was as though we had communication, he and I, through thought and silence, instead of words.

The day wore on and still I did not speak to anyone. Then in the middle of the afternoon, my seat mate asked if he might tell me that he recognized me. I was reluctant to acknowledge recognition, but I have never been able to lie comfortably and it was not worth the effort now, and so I thanked him, and said yes, it was I. It became necessary then to talk politely and casually, but I could still be solitary, not mentioning the reason why I was here, and I asked him about himself. I do not remember his name, it seems impossible to remember anything specific about that journey, and I doubt I would recognize his face again if I saw him. He was tall, because I had to look up when I spoke, and he had a lean western sort of face. The one thing I do remember was that he was traveling for the Wells Fargo Bank and that roused a vague historical interest. Wells Fargo is a romantic name in American history, but of banking I know nothing beyond the needs of every day.

Encouraged by my ignorance, the traveler explained to me with a dry vivid clarity exactly what his task was, and I grasped the significance of international banking, particularly in our modern world. He had been to Singapore and Hong Kong and other cities that I knew well, but he saw them in a light entirely new to me, in areas unknown, where men manipulate the exchange of currencies and provide capital and create power as they see fit. I listened with an interest that was first listless and then superficial and finally real, "the irresistible need to explore." I forgot myself, almost, and was surprised when the voice of the radio over our heads announced that we had arrived in Honolulu. I saw then that it was night again. We had run through a whole day in a short space of time and were once more entering our own country.

The usual bustle of disembarking and lining up for customs inspection took place and I do not remember that. What I do remember was again an experience. For while I waited, deeply aware again of being alone, a customs official came to me and asked me to step aside. I did so, and he leaned across the counter to speak in a low voice.

"I don't want to hold you up, but there's something I want to talk about, confidentially."

I was surprised out of myself again. I had never seen this man before, a big burly fellow, a kind round face, very American.

"You see," he said, his voice low, "I have a retarded daughter."

Ah, now I knew why he had drawn me aside! I am accustomed to having people take me aside and tell me this. Everywhere in the world I have had the same experience. "I want to tell you—I have a child—"

"Tell me about her," I said.

I listened while he talked, and though I heard every familiar word, I was filled with inner wonder. How could it be that at this very moment when I needed desperately to be made to want to live, this man should be here, recalling me to life? For much of my life has been spent in working with and for those who are the parents of retarded children and for their children. This has been my destiny. Yet in the last hours, ever since my daughter's voice had come to me over the telephone in the early morning in Tokyo, I had not once remembered this part of my life. Now here it was, claiming me again.

"You see," the man was saying, "it's this way. My wife and I are having an argument. She says that Americans always put their retarded children into institutions because it's better for them there. And she says that we ought to be doing what Americans do, now that Hawaii is a state. And I say that our girl is no trouble—she's gentle and quiet and she'd be lonesome in an institution."

"Would your wife be happier if she were there?" I asked.

"No, she cries when she talks about it but she says it would be better for the girl."

"Do you want her there?"

"Me? It would break my heart."

I considered. "What would happen if both of you happened to die? Who would take care of your daughter?"

"Plenty! My wife's Hawaiian. She's got one of these big Hawaiian families. They'd all take care of our girl. Matter of fact, they get mad when we talk about an institution. It's just that my wife—"

"Tell your wife she is wrong and the rest of you are right," I said. "Your daughter is lucky. She has a family who wants to keep her. I am sure that American parents in your circumstances would wish they were as lucky as you and your wife in having such a family."

His honest face cleared. "Thanks," he said.

He led me back to the luggage station. "Anything to declare?"

"Nothing," I said. It was true. I had nothing.

"Okay," he said, and marked my bags with chalk and smiled at me. "So long," he said. "I'll never forget you. This is my lucky day. Wait till I tell my wife. She won't believe me. It's a miracle."

It was a miracle for me, too.

And then, as though to test me, I was alone again. I had never traveled alone before his illness. Traveling had always been a gay business for us. He was a delightful traveling companion. He always knew what there was to see, and where we should go and I went with him in careless happiness. Now I had to find the restaurant and get something to eat. We had been given dinner tickets. But where was one to go? I wandered about, feeling stupidly helpless and shy. When a woman has always been accompanied by a cheerful, knowledgeable man, to be suddenly alone is a bewilderment. I wandered the wrong way, asked someone and went in the opposite direction and arrived too late in the restaurant and saw no available seat. I was about to leave again and think no more of food, when a pleasant-looking American approached me and asked if I were looking for a place to sit, and if so, there was one over yonder—two, in fact, if I didn't mind having dinner with him.

I accepted with relief and he led the way to a small half-hidden table. We sat down, he ordered dinner, and I was grateful. The inner solitude was invincible and permanent, I knew that, but it was as if somewhere he saw my predicament and since he could not be with me, he sent strangers in his place. I asked this stranger's name. He gave it to me and told me he was a scientist and had been sent from Washington to work with other scientists in Japan. Again part of my life reclaimed me. Science, especially nuclear physics, has long been my avocation, and I listened now with understanding and interest, quite detached from my inner self. The Japanese, he told me, were excellent scientists, and in particular they know more about the ionosphere than any other scientists in the world. The ionosphere, that state of the upper atmosphere where, as Clyde Orr says, "radiations produce a witch's brew of metastable molecules and ions, atomic entities having electric charges," (*Between Earth and Space*, page 21). It is the birthplace of electricity, the source of electric storms, against which the energy stored in the earth plays an eternal duet of contrapuntal violence. Again my mind was stirred by irresistible curiosity and I was reminded, as though he, wherever he was now, had reminded me that life could go on in these interests which we had shared. An hour passed and the voice came over the radio bidding us take our seats in the jet again. Somehow the day had passed and three times a human being had been sent to speak to me, help me, and remind me of life.

Night fell once more. I did not know what night to call it, a nameless night, since time had stretched itself longer than its name. I had lived twenty-four hours beyond the span between Sunday night and Monday morning. I had made the initial step into my future life. This night I slept, fitfully but without fear. No one could take his place, he would not expect that, nor could I, but strangers would come when I needed them, and I could learn of them and let them go, because another would come. It was like the universal motion of all life, the waves of energy that beat about our globe, made up of innumerable separate particles. What are human beings but particles, and we come and go, too, ceaselessly, in waves of motion and substance. My life was now part of the whole, a separate particle, alone and apart, yet drawn inescapably into the surge and withdrawal of the human tide.

When next dawn came it was to pour its golden light upon the landscape of America. The voice on the radio announced that we would now begin the descent over the city of Allentown in Pennsylvania. Allentown is only a few miles from my farmhouse home. Did the children dream that I was passing by, but far above them in the clouds? I made a hasty toilet, drank coffee, and then we came swiftly down and down, and I saw the gleaming towers of New York.

Now friends had to be faced again and family and for a moment I dreaded it. It had been easier here in the shelter of those who knew nothing about my journey and why I made it. I had told no one, and so needed not to meet the strain of sympathy. It was time now, however, to meet my children and especially to accept their help. In comforting me, they too would be comforted.

The morning was fair. Sunshine poured through the mists as I walked across the airfield into the port. There inside the door my dear and only sister and two of my daughters waited and with them the faithful Pennsylvania Dutchman who has driven my cars for many years. I looked into each face and whatever I had dreaded melted away. I had been wrong—it was good to be with those who knew me and loved me and whom I loved. I am rich in three sons and six daughters, of these six, the eldest is the child who never grew, to whom I owe so much, and five others ranging from my competent, professional, occupational-therapist daughter to the gentle half-American child of eleven who came to me from Japan. The two youngest daughters are half-Japanese, their fathers, American soldiers. The next, lively and an organizer, is half-German, her father American, too. The little middle one, the married one with three perfect babies, is the one who lives across the brook from me, the one with dark hair, big violet eyes and a fiery temper, softened by a quick sense of humor. Each son has his individual strength, each daughter her peculiar grace, each an indispensable place in my life. But today I was glad the three younger daughters were at home and that the middle and older ones were here to meet me with my sister, three strong and understanding women.

Of course we were close, closer than we had ever been even in our happy life together. His death quickened every bond between us. Nor did I overlook the quiet understanding of our driver. He took my baggage checks and led us to the car and we got in and waited for him. In a few minutes we were on our way home, through the streets of New York to the Lincoln Tunnel and the Turnpike. It was all familiar and safe, a journey I had made hundreds of times through the years, at first always with him, and in the last five years alone. It had taken seven years for his strong body and fine brain to end their span on earth.

And what fun it had been from the very beginning, how satisfying the years together! We had begun in New York, where his life had been for thirty years before we met. The first winter we lived in a cosmopolitan hotel in a suite of pleasant rooms and it had not been strange to me, for with people passing to and fro from all parts of the world, it might have been a hotel in Shanghai or Peking. And the next year, when we adopted our first two babies, we moved to a terraced apartment, and began our life as parents. He had always wanted a big family and how we enjoyed its gradual accumulation! Two years slipped by, and they held nothing but joy and content, and we took two more babies. Then his next dream, which was to live in the country, became a necessity. Four small children can scarcely be contained successfully in any apartment. My own childhood had been spent in a spacious old tropical bungalow, surrounded by gardens and beyond the wall the hills and fields outside the city of Chinkiang, in Kiangsu province, a port city on the great Yangtze River. I could not imagine a child growing up on cement among towers, however beautiful, for in its city way I love New York. We moved then to our farm home, and he devoted himself, as he had always hoped he could, to editorial work. He was a reluctant business man, and had his brilliance been only a little more channeled, he might have been a writer of books. As it was, he wrote a few as varied as he was himself, the clever rhymes for children, a humorous mystery novel, a fine nonfiction work on Marco Polo, simplified again for young people and published by Random House in the Landmark Series, and a critical study of Buffalo Bill, a character in whom he took much skeptical interest.

As the years passed, the farmhouse developed into a rambling comfortable home for an increasing family. He taught the children tennis and baseball and golf and they learned early to swim and to ride. I was busy at my own work, but the big window of my study opens toward the swimming pool, and I could see by instinct when a child grew too adventuresome. Our life was organized casually around work and children and we lived deeply. Our pleasures were in music and people and children and books and the world of woods and mountain and sea.

I do not know whether it is easier to have the end come suddenly or gradually over the years. I think, if I had been given the choice, I would have preferred a sudden end, shock and all. Then memory would not be entangled with the slow and agonizing fading of perception and speech and at last recognition even of those loved and dear. There is, however, one balm. He did not know of his own decline. And as he was reduced to the elemental physical aspects of his life, his essential nature remained, as I have said, what it had always been, an unselfish sweetness.

Slowly, slowly, the change came. When his eyes failed and he could no longer read, we sent for the records of books. I must here express my permanent gratitude to the Library of Books for the Blind. They kept a continuing stream of records coming into the house, free of charge, and his brain was kept alive and stimulated beyond what we had feared. But this too came to an end. The day came when words ceased to have their meaning, and even music faded, and he was content merely to exist. He would have suffered had he known, and I thank a kind intelligence, wherever it is, that he never knew. The body lived on, relieved of any strain of mind or spirit or emotion, and assumed a strange durability of its own.

"This will last a long time," our family doctor said again. "You must go on about your usual work. You must live, you must travel, you must not let yourself be absorbed by this which cannot be helped."

And indeed it was the only way to endure what was happening to us. I tried to live as usual, insofar as I could.

The end had come quite unexpectedly. I listened as my dark-haired daughter talked while we drove homeward through the green countryside of late spring. Everything had been the same with him until two days before. She came across the brook with her three little children after breakfast, on her morning visit. She found him awake and ready for the day. The children climbed on his bed and kissed him and stroked his cheeks. He provided, I think, an element of total security in their lives. He was always there in bed, had been ever since they were born, and they had no memories of his being different. They went away again, and when she returned a little later he was gone. It was so simple a story that I could bear to hear it told. For a long time he had not known he was living and he did not know when he died.

"There was nothing anyone could have done," my daughter told me.

"I know," I said. "I have known that for a long time."

I could feel nothing for the moment but finality, an immense weariness of mind and body, now that I knew all there was to know. I suppose two nights of broken sleep and the strain of being myself, insofar as possible, even among strangers, had been more wearing than I knew. I sat in silence, my hands in my daughter's warm young grasp. The car drove up the familiar driveway at last. The kind people who help me in house and offices and grounds were waiting. There had to be meeting, the acceptance of their tears and sympathy, and then the freedom to go to my own room. All our children were at home, gathered from everywhere. They had done everything. His room which for so long had been a hospital was already a guest room. The hospital bed was gone, carpets were fresh and clean, crisp white curtains hung at the windows. My room was immaculate and cheerful with roses. I saw everything and felt nothing. I was walking in my sleep. When anyone stopped talking for a moment, I fell asleep. After luncheon, which I suppose I ate, but I cannot remember, I lay on the couch in the living room, I who am never exhausted, and while the children planned, I slept. It was not like any sleep I have ever known. I simply fell into unconsciousness.

The next two days center upon three events. We went, all of us, to tell him our last good-by. Of course it was only his body we saw. He was not there. But the body is precious. Through the body we express our love and with the body we live. I remember my mother one day when I was a small child, not more than seven. I was desperately ill with diphtheria in a Chinese city. My younger brother had just died of the same disease, and they were burying him that day, and my mother was sobbing. A friend, well-intentioned but without understanding, reproached her.

"It is only his body," she told my mother. "His soul is in heaven with Our Lord."

My mother flew into anger, sobs and all. "But his body is precious," she cried. "I gave it birth. I tended it and loved it. Wherever his soul is, it is out of my reach, and they are taking his body away, and it is all I have."

These words came back to me as I stood by his beloved body. He lay on a couch, his eyes closed and his hands loosely at his sides. He wore his tweed suit, the one he liked, a blue-gray, and the dark blue tie I had given him last Christmas. His beautiful hair, only partly white, was brushed as he always wore it, back from his forehead. His face was young again, the lines gone, the lips tranquil. I kissed his cheek. I touched his hand that had always been warm and quick to respond. The flesh was cold.

The next day we had the simple service that the children had planned. They had moved to one side the furniture in the library and in midmorning, when the sun was pouring into the courtyard, and the small fountain, a little stone boy from Italy, was playing gently into the pool, I stood at my bedroom window. The men were bringing him home for the last time. When I came downstairs our household people and those on the farm, the children and their families and the nurses who had cared for him, were waiting for me. The men had set his coffin before the chimney piece. The lid was closed. Our family minister read aloud from such books as he deemed fitting. Then he spoke a few words of friendship. I do not remember what he said. I sat thinking of the many hours we had spent in this room. It had first been the children's playroom. Then when they grew big enough to want basketball and roller-skating we made the barn into their play place and designed this room into the family library, lined with bookshelves. Above the chimney piece he hung a painting of an illustration of a story by John Galsworthy, which he had published in *Collier's* when he was editor of that magazine. It is a beautiful painting in oils, evocative and poetic. The story was the first ever published in America, I believe, by Galsworthy. It is about a young novice in a nunnery, upon the last night of her novitiate. She must make up her mind in these final hours whether she will become a nun or return to life and to her lover. By chance a beautiful dancer takes shelter for the night in the nunnery and after the evening meal she dances for the nuns. The artist paints her dancing, her long scarlet skirt floating about her. In the foreground the little novice sits entranced and, as the story goes, she ran away that night to join her lover and live her woman's life as wife and mother. The picture has always hung there above the oak-paneled chimney piece and it hangs there now.

As for the books, he took great care that they were properly classified in their own alcoves: fiction, social science biographies, children's books, travel books, new books, and so on. He was a lover of books, a cultivated and world-minded man. Well and deeply as I knew Asia, he could tell me facts that I did not know. When once we visited India and Southeast Asia, and China and Japan, he knew all the important people whom we should meet, and he could tell me the history of every sight we saw. He was a charming and interesting companion at home and abroad. Above all, he never condescended to me as man to woman.

I went upstairs to my own room again as they carried him away and this somehow was the worst moment and still is. He was leaving our house and our home and forever. And then came the long drive to his family cemetery in New York, where his parents are buried. Yes, everyone was kind. Those whose duty it was to tend him on this last journey were thoughtful and quiet and when we neared the end of the journey, policemen led us through traffic to our destination.

I pause here, remembering. And what do I remember? This—in the midst of that sorrowful ride, every moment of it concentrated agony so that my very bones ached, I chanced to see from the rear window, and against my will, the long slow procession of black cars. Yes, but at the very end were two other cars. They were station wagons and they were fire-engine red. I recognized them immediately. One belonged to my second son and one to my equally youthful son-in-law. I had winced when they brought them to show me proudly before I went to Japan and heroically I had admired them. Now here they were, bright and alive in the morning sun. I knew why—and my heart dissolved again in tears and laughter. What a shame, what a pity, that he could not see those two shining red station wagons, doing him honor upon this occasion—and how he would have laughed!

Why do I say would have? It is possible that somewhere you were laughing. It is still possible. I maintain my stand, until—

Everything was ready for us when we arrived in the quiet place. The birds were singing and flowers were blooming. It did not take long to perform the final ceremony of giving his body back to the earth. Our minister had come with us and he spoke the final words of peace and acceptance. My sons and my stepson stood beside me, strong young men, the stepson to carry on his father's firm. My daughters walked with me back to the car and we drove away . . . But oh, that silent last moment, when he must be left behind, and the arrival at the house, now empty! Of these I cannot speak. To other women in like circumstances, who may read these pages, I can only say there is no escape from such moments when they come. They must be lived through, not once but many times in memory. I have been told that they grow easier. I do not find it so. I come back to my home as to a haven whenever I leave it, but it is not the same, and it will never be the same. I know that now. Since there is no escape from the fact, there can only be acceptance. And acceptance comes at last, but not at once—oh, never at once.

I should not, I suppose, have gone to Vermont. But we have always gone there when the summer gets too hot in Pennsylvania. It can grow very hot, for, as someone has said, this State is "the far thin edge of the tropics." Our woods and fields grow lush as any jungle, and the nights stay hot. Perhaps I felt that I could escape, somehow, from his continuing absence. It took me long to learn how impossible that is, wherever I go in the world. At any rate, after a few weeks I took my three younger daughters with me to Vermont. Years ago, when it became settled that ragweed and I could not exist together, I built a three-room house for him and for me—two bedrooms and a big living room which was also a dining room with a cooking counter. Here he and I had spent good summers, and the children had rooms over the garage for their own. Into this house that had been his and mine, I now went alone, and the girls took the rooms over the garage. I set myself to writing and I practiced my piano, and spent hours on the high terrace facing Stratton Mountain. I do not know why I imagined that anything would be easier here. For one thing, I could not write. My mind, lost in thought and memory and question, simply would not busy itself with the creation of other people's lives. I was as remote from everyone as though it were I who had died. No, it would not do. Vermont was not the place. And for once I needed another employment than writing. I needed work that I had to do, work with others, compelling me daily to rise early and go to an appointed place where it was my duty to be.

When this conviction dawned upon me I made up my mind. I would go back to Japan and resume my work on the picture. My co-workers had been busy. They had found locations, a fishing village which they thought ideal for our picture, a terraced farm, an empty beach, a fisherman's house, a gentleman's house. The volcano we had. They were ready for me to return to the job. When was I coming? I said, immediately. It was nearing the end of August. The girls would go back to school soon, and they could live with their elder sister. There was no family reason to hold me at home and I welcomed the thought of work and Japan.

Two

THE ATMOSPHERE INTO which I descended once more from the jet on the airfield near Tokyo was one of welcome and quiet unspoken sympathy. The deeper the feelings, the Japanese believe, the less should be spoken. We Americans find it necessary to speak, to send letters and cards of condolence. Hundreds of letters had poured into my office before I left home and I had read them all because it was good to know in what esteem he was held and in so many places in the world. And people, friends or strangers, had stopped me on streets and country roads to tell me. "I am so sorry to hear—"

In Tokyo nothing was said, yet everything was conveyed. Consideration was delicate but complete. My room in the hotel was bright with flowers and baskets of fruit. The little maids were ever present and solicitous. I understood, for in Japan even love is not to be expressed in words. There are no such words as "I love you" in the Japanese language.

"How do you tell your husband that you love him?" I once asked a Japanese friend.

She looked slightly shocked. "An emotion as deep as love between husband and wife cannot be put into words. It must be expressed in attitude and act."

Nor are there Japanese equivalents of our love words—sweetheart, darling, dear, and all the rest. Certain young Japanese are beginning to use the English words, but even they not seriously, perhaps. But perhaps again no one uses these words seriously any more. I hear American directors scattering them carelessly and casually upon the loved and the unloved alike, in the fashion of Hollywood and Broadway, and I always remonstrate. To a writer all words are significant and valuable, individual words as well as words in association, each to be used only in its fitting place, like jewels. The English language is peculiarly rich in the words of love, their roots deep in ancient Anglo-Saxon soil. To hear a man call a secretary or an actress or perhaps only a girl whose name he does not remember by the precious words of love always makes me—well, angry! It is a desecration of true feeling, the deepest in the human heart. For me nothing in life equals or even resembles in value and treasure true love between man and woman, with all it implies. The words we have used for centuries to express this love are not to be tarnished, for they belong to all of us. If they are tarnished by careless misuse, how shall we express true love? We are robbed of something that cannot be replaced. Any woman who has heard the man she loves call her his sweetheart, his darling, his love, can only be profoundly angered when these words are destroyed.

"How can you misuse these words?" I demanded of an American.

He laughed, uncomprehending. "It makes the girls feel good," he said lightly. "It's informal—like—you know—friendly."

The Japanese girls did not feel "good" about it, nor did they consider it friendly. Those few who did were problems. They thought that love words meant love, and they became serious and consequently troublesome. The others, who were not looking for love from American men, with consequent benefits, considered such an American unduly interested in sex and therefore insulting. It took explanations before they could be placated. They were usually too polite to complain in his presence but behind his back what scorn!

"I'll sue him if he says it again," a young actress exclaimed, her black eyes bright with fury . . . And sue him she did. Yes, we had our problems.

Our locations were set, although I had not yet seen them except on film; the next task was to find our cast. Since the story of *The Big Wave* is altogether Japanese, the cast was to be Japanese, and we had already engaged a Japanese crew and cameraman. For the first time an American film company was making a picture in Japan, co-produced by a Japanese film company, the largest and in some ways the best, and with Japanese crew and cameraman. It was an experiment, a profoundly interesting one. I had seen motion pictures made before of my books, but none like this, and with me. I did not intend to interfere with directing or in any of the professional aspects, for I know my areas of ignorance, but I was to have the privilege of being anywhere I liked, and to speak when I wished. On the whole, I believed my fellow workers had confidence in my ability to be silent. I would not speak much or often. I am, in fact, a quiet woman by nature, unless oppressed by what I consider injustice when I become, I am told, excruciatingly articulate.

Certainly I enjoyed sitting in on the casting. We were given office space in the handsome building owned by our Japanese co-producers, and each day I went there early and stayed late, looking, listening, judging, disapproving or approving, while those in command gave auditions to actors and actresses, adults and children. Our first concern was to find the children, two boys, two girls, who were to begin the story. Therefore children came to us, accompanied by mothers.

I have seen many stage children, and they can be sad children. These Japanese stage children, however, were not sad. They were like all other Japanese children, healthy and happy and exuding a general atmosphere of being much loved. Neither they nor their mothers were tense, as so many of our American stage children and mothers are tense, which difference I can only ascribe to the possibility that competition is not as important in Japanese life as it is in ours, and the desire to excel is second to the consideration of human feelings.

They came in, one after the other, each mother unobtrusively following her particular star, and they bowed with the grace bestowed by that extra hinge which seems to have developed in the Japanese back. It is unique, this bow. The

Chinese bobs his head cheerfully at greeting and parting and the Korean makes a proud inclination. The Japanese performs obeisance, deep but also proud.

Only one boy in the endless procession seemed reluctant or rebellious. He came in early one morning, flanked by his mother and his aunt, the only boy who needed the escort of two women and it soon became evident why. He was a handsome fellow, but sulky, his bow was just short of courtesy and at first he would not talk. His mother and his aunt, in gentle distress and apology for such behavior, informed us eagerly that he was a champion swimmer. This was good, the part called for a good swimmer and we congratulated the boy, who only continued to look sulky. We invited him to sit down and he sat down, still sulky. He condescended, after several whispered pleadings from his lady relatives, to answer our questions briefly—too briefly—all the time staring at the wall. Yes, he said in answer to direct question, he was in school—Japanese school. Yes, he did speak English—sometimes. He had been three and a half years in Cairo, Egypt, and there he went to English school but he preferred not to speak English. . . . He liked Japanese school better than English school. . . . He did not wish to remember Cairo. Well, it was a city, and that's all. . . . He grew more and more sulky. Something occurred to us. We put a final question.

"Do you want to be in this motion picture?"

He lifted his head, his face brightened for the first time. He shouted.

"No!"

We put one more arrow question. "Do you ever want to be an actor?"

He shone now like a neon light. "No!"

We burst into laughter and he looked at us hopefully.

"The interview is over," we told him, "and you are a wise man. You know what you don't want."

He tramped out, unsmiling, a lordly male, his female relatives trotting after him, pained but acquiescent. It was obvious that he had won a family victory and that he was accustomed to such victories.

Days passed and the actors narrowed down to the impossibles and the possibles, the latter by far the smaller group. Japan has many excellent actors of both sexes and all ages, but we were looking for excellent actors who also spoke English, since the dialogue was to be in English. At first we hoped, unrealistically, that their English would be perfect. Later we merely hoped their English could be understood well enough so that it could give the illusion of Japanese.

Which illusion reminds me of an incident of my own life in China. I was stopping to rest one day at a wayside inn in a remote province. An old woman came to pour tea into my bowl. I thanked her in Chinese and asked her how she did. She stared at me in terror and dropped the teapot. "The gods save me," she gasped. "What is the matter with me? I can understand English!"

Something of this we hoped to achieve, but there were times when we wondered if we were fools to hope. The variety of accents in English-speaking Japanese is astounding but they have one characteristic in common. The consonant "L" seems foreign to the Japanese ear as well as to the Japanese tongue.

In such diverting work the day passed until evening fell, and the trouble with every day was that at the end of it there was always night.

For the first time in my life I was sad when evening came. The others went to their husbands and wives, but I came back alone to my hotel room. The windows looked over the roofs of new Tokyo—as I have said, not beautiful, for there has not been time enough to create beauty. The city was hastily rebuilt after the war, a pity, for after it was thoroughly flattened by bombing it would have been well, if possible, to design a city with wide streets and parkways, a modern city but beautiful in the Japanese fashion. It was not done. The war had been harsh, people were desperate to begin living again, and the government was all but bankrupt. Houses went up helter-skelter. Today it is still almost impossible to find a house by its number or even by its street. One can only entrust one's self to the unknown.

Evenings in lonely hotel rooms are impossible, at least for me. I had friends in plenty, and invitations in plenty, more than I could accept, but these did not fill the need. One had always to maintain a front, or a poise, and this could be done during the day's work when the mind was engaged. It was different when one had to respond individually to others. In despair and loneliness I took to wandering the streets at night, unknown and free. Tokyo is rich in theaters and motion picture houses and usually I stopped by in one or the other. Though I did not understand the dialogue, the drift of the story was easy to catch, and I could be mildly amused, superficially at least, by what I saw. The houses were always packed, the audiences grave and intense until a comic moment brought loud, staccato laughter, stopped instantaneously by intent gravity again.

On one such evening I chanced to see an American woman of about my own age wandering as I was wandering. We stopped, startled each by the other, then I spoke. She was from Los Angeles, her husband had gone to Formosa, where she did not wish to follow, her daughter had a dinner date with a young American man, and she was indulging in a long-concealed wish to wander about Tokyo alone. By this time, however, she looked uncertain, though not frightened, and I proposed that we see the picture together, which we did, to our mutual enjoyment. The acquaintance ripened into a friendship, and later a dinner with her family, and another still later in Los Angeles. The point of this incident is that I did not realize how an American woman looks in a Japanese crowd. When I saw her, I forgot, of course, how I also looked among thousands of Japanese.

I had, actually, a warmly comfortable feeling when I was alone in a Japanese crowd. This must have been a lingering memory of the atmosphere of my childhood when, accompanied by my Chinese nurse, I sat in a Chinese theater or out-of-doors on a village threshing floor or in a temple courtyard, to watch a play. The play was always the thing in China, and the star system was unknown, unless of course one went to Shanghai, or Peking, there to attend the performance of such as star as, for example, Mei Lan-fang, or Butterfly Wu. As a child I had no such privilege, but I enjoyed the miracle plays and the long historical dramas through which the Chinese everyday folk learned religion, philosophy and the history of their own people. They accepted me as a frequent member of the audience, and I lost myself, a fair-haired American child in the Asian multitude—a kindly multitude in those days and I was never held responsible for the sins of colonialism as all white folk are nowadays and by all Asians, it seems. I was conscious only of being surrounded by pleasant and humorous people. In Tokyo now I found the same people, though of a different nation and country, and they accepted me merely because they had become used to Americans as part of the world landscape. They know the best and the worst of us from the long years of the Occupation and we cannot surprise them any more, either by good or evil.

Tokyo has, of course, its darker aspects. There were streets in which I did not enjoy walking alone any more than I do in certain parts of New York and Philadelphia where I have learned that it is dangerous not only so to walk, but also even to ride with the doors of my car unlocked. Cities are cities and hooligans are to be found in all.

Those were the days, too, of the student riots in Tokyo, about which we North Americans had so much misinformation. I can only say that I was there, that I saw the crowds of young men and women, earnest, determined, informed. They were not anti-American. They were Japanese who liked their constitution although it had been engineered by Americans—at least by an American. They liked especially the part in which Japan as a nation promises never again to wage war. Now they, the Japanese, were being asked by Americans to take sides in case of war and with the West, although they were oriented toward Asia, and in the future must in common sense be a neutral people. With American bases on their soil they felt themselves forced to be partisan. It amounted to a situation which to them became unendurable in its confusion. The Japanese are a well-organized people, they have their different levels, they do not confuse their best selves with their worst. Whatever level they stand upon temporarily, it is that one and no other. Therefore they went on riot to proclaim their confusion, but they did not hate anybody. In confusion they are capable of assassination, not out of hatred necessarily, but merely to clear up confusion.

Students have always been an alarming and exciting and interesting part of my life. I do not mean the relatively placid students of North America, whose most active moments seem to demonstrate nothing more violent or even exciting than college pranks. I am accustomed to the students of Japan and India, Korea and Japan. In China the new age, whatever it was and we had new ages with bewildering and rapid change, was always announced by an uprising of students. The people respected these young men and women because they were persons who, if not learned, were nevertheless in pursuit of learning and therefore more privileged and presumably better informed than the average citizen who could not read or write. Books, the Asian peoples believe, are treasure houses of human wisdom and since students alone had access to books, the position of a student in Asia carried, and still carries, a prestige far out of proportion to age and class. They were a devoted group and risked death in every uprising. During the Nationalist regime in China I had seen many of them killed for being suspected of Communism. Doubtless some of them were Communists but most of them were simply dedicated young patriots, desperately desiring to better the conditions under which their people lived. They are the unnumbered and unnamed martyrs but they cannot be discounted, for all of that. If one wants to know what is about to happen in an Asian country, watch the students.

As for the picture, while all this was going on, we needed a tidal wave. Everything else we could find but the tidal wave could not be summoned at will. The story itself began in a tidal wave. Once, when I was spending a year in Japan on the island of Kyushu, I had become acquainted with a small and lovely fishing village on the southern tip of the coast. A dozen or so stone cottages were huddled together behind a stone sea wall. The houses had no doors, no windows, toward the sea. It was not that the fishing folk did not love the sea. They did indeed, for generations of the families had lived beside it and by it. Yet generations had known, too, the fury of those vast waves that rise out of earthquakes under the sea. Volcano and sea work together for death and I had seen them so work one bright September day. There had been premonitions. The water in the deep well, the fisherfolk told me, had been muddy for a few days. The well, dug in the beach, was only a few feet from the sea and at the foot of a high cliff, but the water was sweet. Thither the village women had walked, a mile each way, to carry all the fresh water the village used, and this for hundreds of years. When I suggested that this might be a hardship the men smiled incredulously. I must say the women did, too.

Earthquake, of course, comes first. The earthquake in Chile had sent a tidal wave rushing across the sea to northwest Japan, but usually the earthquake is in Japan, or under the sea nearby. Earthquake—I cannot even say the word to myself as I sit here upon the solid earth of my Pennsylvania farm home without a touch of that bottomless sickness of heart and body, that organic dismay, which falls upon a human being when the earth quakes beneath his feet. It is as if the very globe were dissolving into space. The one security we humans have is this earth which is our home, this globe to which we cling. Catastrophe befalls us, thunder and lightning roar and flash in the sky, winds come down from outer space, rain falls in torrents from the clouds, even the sea may rise in storm, but underneath everything we have the earth, or feel we have. We may have been spawned from the sea but we are land creatures now. When the land betrays us, when we cannot stand upon our feet, when the ground splits and swallows our homes and our people, then we are lost indeed. . . . Once in a violent earthquake in Japan the earth split and a running child fell into the chasm. The mother pursued her child and leaped in after him, and the earth closed again, leaving only her long black hair to lie like seaweed on the quivering surface. . . .

The second day after I came back to Tokyo, as I was writing at the desk in my hotel room, after midnight, I felt that deep troubled tremor of the earth and once more the old sickness rose in me. The quake was no more than a tremor and yet for that instant my hand went out of control, and the desk shook. Most of the people slept through it, but the morning newspaper reported a sharp tremor. Such tremors come often in Japan, hundreds, thousands of them in a year, on the average of four times a day, and each time it is a reminder to a courageous people that they live on dangerous islands. The effect on them of this eternal tension is obvious. They have extremes of temperament—an exaggerated gaiety, a profound and sometimes frenzied melancholy. A disciplined and studied surface, smiles and calm and casualness, is underlaid, without exception, I might say, by a dark sadness, born of the knowledge in child and adult that catastrophe is endemic in spite of the beauty of mountain and sea and the kindliness of life. This universal knowledge begets in them a consideration, a tender courtesy, as though to say that since the world may end at any moment, let us be kind to one another. When this inherent kindness has to be unlearned, as it does in times of war, when men must be taught to be brutal, they may be cruel beyond imagination . . . But I was speaking of earthquakes—and tidal waves.

We needed a tidal wave then. The earthquake we could reproduce by camera, but the tidal wave was beyond us. It was here that we had good fortune. Our Japanese co-producers had the finest special-effects studio in the country and, I was told, in the world. I did not know what special effects meant in film talk, but I discovered that it meant the reproduction, in miniature, of a scene in nature. The Japanese are supremely talented in such work and of all Japanese, Tsuburaya is the most talented. Fortunately Tsuburaya belonged to our Japanese co-producers and upon appointment we met him in their offices.

He is an artist and the first look at him revealed the fact. He wore work clothes, baggy pants, baggy shirt and a Japanese coat, and he greeted us with a charmingly natural courtesy. Yes, he said, he knew that we wanted a tidal wave and he had already make sketches to show us. They were startlingly accurate water colors of the rising horizon, the onrushing wave, and the towering crash of the crest. A tidal wave does not appear at first as a wave. Instead the horizon lifts, the sea mounts toward the sky in a smoooth brimming line, it runs toward the land, a wall of water that may be two feet high or two hundred. A powerful suction gathers the sea into the wave, so that watching from a cliff, the bottom of the ocean beyond the beach is laid bare. Then the gigantic wave curls over its own base and overwhelms land, house and people.

I watched Tsuburaya's face as he described the sequences he had painted. I wish I could paint this beautiful Japanese face, even in words. I say beautiful in the deep sense of the word. It was not handsome, in the superficial sense. It was worn with thought and concentration. It was as sensitive as a child's face, a genius child, but not in the least childish. It was wise and gentle, yet fresh and strong and humorous, the face of an artist purified by the satisfaction of fulfillment through his art. We talked quietly. I listened while he described his plans. He would come to the fishing village with his cameraman and photograph everything. Then he would build the sets in the studio and recreate the scenes and adapt them to the film. This would be done later, when work was in progress. Meanwhile I had the private content of the writer who knows that work is understood and is about to be translated truthfully into another medium.

I have learned by experience that people who work in the theater are not to be judged by the standards applied to the rest of us. They are a group apart, by temperament, whatever their race, class or nationality. A Chinese actor, male or female, is like an American actor, and is like an actor of any other country because they are, first of all, actors. Directors are the same, whatever their age, color, religion, nationality, all prima donnas, without a single exception. I make this general observation as preliminary to our first real problem in making the picture. Everything had gone so pleasantly, so easily, that I might have expected, cheerful pessimist that I am, a storm on the horizon, a knot in the thread, a hitch in the machinery.

It came one hot summer morning when the air conditioning had broken down—in order to provide the proper temperature for coming storm, I suppose. The production manager approached me with an exaggerated courtesy. We were in his office as usual, the American director and I, and the production manager had been too cordial for safety. I should have known he had an idea. He ordered several pretty girls to bring us tea, and when the American said he preferred coffee, because this was the only place in Tokyo which had good coffee, the production manager shouted at another bevy of pretty girls to bring coffee. When we were all seated about the low round table, and after he had swabbed the perspiration from his well-nourished face and neck, he said, too casually, that since his firm's reputation was also staked on our picture, they would like to supply a Japanese assistant director to the American.

I know that nothing in life is really casual. Hence when I saw a sudden alert in the American's eyes, I made my reply casual. Of course, I said, we would welcome such aid. I wanted the picture to be true in every detail. It would be expected in my own country. The production manager mentioned even more casually the name of a director. I recognized it. It was the name of a famous Japanese film director now officially retired but still inexhaustibly a director.

"I would like to meet him," the American director said also casually.

Everything seemed smooth and civilized, the production manager sighed happily and insisted on ginger ale in addition to the tea and coffee. He was a big man, tall and heavy, and he was temperamental. Indeed, I had been taken aside privately the day before we met and warned that he and the American director might not get on well, their natures not being in harmony. I inquired as to what this meant. It was explained to me in Japanese terms that the American was full of energy and determination, and so was the Japanese. The American did not easily yield on a point on which he considered himself right. Neither did the Japanese. Let us say bluntly that neither ever yielded. I had been disturbed by this, and now it occurred to me that a Japanese assistant director might act as a buffer.

When I mentioned this possibility to the American director, however, later in the day, he said shortly that he wanted no buffers. He liked the Japanese production manager because he was as frank as an American and so he could deal with him. I heard an edge in the American director's voice, and I postponed further discussion. I reminded myself that time takes care of many things. Asia had taught me that.

Meanwhile the casting went on, no matter what else took place, a process not different in Tokyo or on Broadway. We sat by invitation behind the long table in the office and one by one actors or actresses appeared in turn. We had their photographs before us and studied them carefully for photogenic quality, while questions were asked.

English was the problem. There were many handsome young men and many, many pretty girls, and some older characters and their female counterparts. The questions were always the same:

"Your name?"

"How many pictures have you made?"

"What do you think was your best part?"

Somewhere in the thick of the questions, usually very soon, it became all too apparent that English was sadly weak, in fact nonexistent. The only perfect English sentence was the same one. "I cannot speak English."

"Where did you study English?" we inquired.

"In school—yes."

"How many years in school?"

"Six yahs."

"Six years?"

A nod. We tried not to smile as these six years were repeated again and again. One of the young men least learned in English said, "Ten yahs."

We tried repeating English words, bits of dialogue. A good ear may make it possible to teach the English dialogue. Sometimes the ear was very good. Usually it was not.

"Next time you make a picture," I advised myself privately, "let's stick to the English-speaking countries."

When at last an actor appeared who spoke perfect English, we tried not to accept him merely because he could speak. There were other requirements. So the days passed, not hopeful and yet not quite hopeless. Meanwhile the matter of the assistant director was not allowed to die. The production manager told us one morning that we were to meet the Japanese director. I was daily more impressed by the production manager, his efficiency and his chronic desperation. He must produce a motion picture every week for Japan's film-hungry population. It was and is an intolerably heavy schedule, but he assured me it could not grow lighter until television improved and provided real competition, when, he said, the motion picture companies would have to produce better pictures and therefore not so many. Meanwhile he could not stop. He carried on conferences with directors, with everybody, it seemed, while he kept a finger in our pie, appearing and reappearing, always in shirt sleeves, his large face shining with sweat in spite of air-conditioned rooms. He had a very handsome face, in the Japanese classical tradition, although not as handsome as it used to be, doubtless, when he was young, before wine and whatever goes with it made its mark. It was too heavy now in the jowls, there were bags under the fine eyes. It lighted easily with laughter, nevertheless, and when he laughed it was with the roar of a lion. He put aside formalities whenever possible and begged us for frankness. He spoke in Japanese, his interpreter one of the pretty young women who softened what he said without destroying its force. She was very skillful. But I still did not really know him. That came later.

One afternoon then, we were led to another office where we were told to wait for our meeting with the proposed Japanese director. We waited. He entered after five minutes or so, looking vaguely like a Japanese Stokowski, but bigger. He was handsome for his age, his white hair swept back, his profile proud. He bowed but not too deeply and I noticed a coldness creep over the face of the American director. Two young men actors were about to create a scene for us. The Japanese director sat down. He understood English as well as the production manager did, but like him, he would not speak it. The American director explained that he wanted the two actors to do a scene between Toru and Yukio, the main characters in *The Big Wave.* The Japanese director seized a pen and began to write down what he thought the scene should be. The American director tried through our interpreter to stop this on the grounds that he did not want the scene to be fixed but fluid. The Japanese silenced her with an imperious wave of the hand. Steel shone in the American's eyes and he instructed the interpreter again.

"Please tell this gentleman I do not want the scene written down. I wish the actors to improvise."

The interpreter, awed by the Japanese director's fame and hauteur, made an effort. Again the imperious wave of the royal hand! The American took over. When the Japanese leaned to give the paper to the actors with his own instructions the American removed it, saying in firm English, "I don't want them to have written instructions."

There was a moment of awed silence on the part of the actors. Whom should they obey? The American, they finally decided, and the Japanese sat back, looking formidable. I knew what was coming, but knew, too, that it must wait until we got back to the hotel. The American maintained perfect manners in public but when the scene was over, rather well done considering the tense atmosphere, we got up, bowed to the Japanese director and everybody else, and took our leave. The interpreter was in the car with us so nothing was said. As we got out, however, at the hotel door, the American spoke to me through clenched teeth. "I must talk with you before everything falls apart."

I bowed to the inescapable. "Very well. Let's have it now, in my rooms. I'll expect you in fifteen minutes."

I needed a few minutes in which to prepare myself for the ordeal of a conference with a prima donna. Define prima donna? Whatever the term is in the dictionary, in real life it means a person self-concentric—not necessarily egoistic or egotistical, and not entirely self-centered, but certainly one the nucleus of whose being is the self. Of directors, there are two kinds, generally speaking; the actor's director, and the director's director. The actor's director is the beloved of actors. He woos them, charms them, defers to them, flatters them, binds them to him emotionally until they do their best for him. He calls this "developing their talents." Sooner or later he also destroys them, especially if they do not release him from the emotional tie he has created between them. He expects to be released as soon as the play opens or the picture is made, for emotion has then served its purpose, and he is indignant if he is not released. Some actors—the females, to be more accurate—are so foolish as to want to continue the tie, and when it is cut off, they are destroyed, at least for a time. Yet so dependent are they in emotional terms that they will continue to speak of him fondly as "an actor's director." The director's director, on the other hand, will avoid the use of emotion as a tool to develop the actor, male or female. He knows what he wants, and will have no truck with "development." He tells the actor exactly what is to be done, in terms of art and the play, and the actor must perform accordingly. Without exception, so far as I know, Japanese directors belong to the latter group.

At this point of my analysis, there was a knock at my door and the American director entered in what is called ominous silence. He sat down and began as usual by pointing out certain minor mistakes I had made during the day—minor or major it did not matter, for by now every mistake was major and all were mine.

"Why," he inquired with frightening distinctness, his eyes gimlets on my face, "did you have to greet that Japanese as though he were an old friend? Why did you have to thank him and say it was good to have his help?"

I muttered something about being polite in the Japanese manner, et cetera, but nothing could stop the inevitable. He did not waver.

"I must tell you," he said, and I knew he must, "that unless this Japanese director is removed at once, I shall return to New York."

I was speechless. Remove the Japanese after the production manager had invited him? It was to be asked to remove Mount Fuji from the landscape of Japan!

The American proceeded in frigid tones. "There can only be one director. It is I—or it is not I."

The sky fell. I was crushed. The crisis I had dreaded had arrived. I had hoped that time would make it less violent, I had been foolishly optimistic and now I was desperate. I am not a good fighter at any time and when faced with a battle, I always try to follow the good old Chinese proverb, "Of the thirty-six ways of escape, the best is to run away." The catch at this moment was that there was no place to run to. I could not run, therefore.

I got up from my chair. It was the end of the day, nearly six o'clock, and I would like to have sent for a pot of Japanese green tea, to which I am addicted, and then, sipping tea, to have read a Japanese novel while I waited for dinner. There was no possibility of either tea or novel. I thought of the worst and most frightening resort and could think of no other. I said,

"Let's go to the production manager's office now and tell him."

I hoped that the American director would admire my courage. It was exactly the same as though I had said let us go to the zoo, find the biggest, fiercest lion and twist his tail. He showed no sign of admiration. He got up and we went, the interpreter timidly behind, paling as we explained our errand.

"Japanese director," she gasped, "is very big man. So is production manager."

It was my turn to pale. I began to hate this American director temporarily. And why did I ever yield to this idea of making a picture in Japan? But I was here. We were already in the building. We were going up in the elevator. We announced ourselves at the door of the production manager's office. Yes, we must see him before he goes, we said. The pretty girl looked surprised, hinted that the production manager was very busy, et cetera, but we said we would wait. We were ushered in and we sat down. The production manager ignored us while he roared into one telephone and another. I noticed foolishly that the telephones were all turquoise blue in a green room. I counted the buttons on a pretty girl's back as she telephoned into still another telephone, repeating the production manager's roars in a gentle voice. Green tea was brought but I dared not try to swallow lest I choke. After a long five minutes, ten minutes, whatever the hours are, the production manager lowered his bulk into one of the circle of chairs and grunted at his interpreter. I understood perfectly that he was asking in his own way why the devil we were there.

I myself wondered. I wished that I were not there, but a glance at the American's grim profile was enough to destroy question and answer. I plunged in, knowing that I was committing suicide. I began by assuring the production manager, who understood every English word I said but pretended he did not, that we were honored by his wish to help us but, under the circumstances, directors being directors, young and old—I meandered on, hoping to avoid the final issue, the last moment, when I must somehow say bluntly that we did not want the Japanese director—that is to say, the American director did not—that is to say, I was sure the production manager understood how embarrassing it would be for an American director making his first picture in Japan, to say to an elder director, one so respected, et cetera. The American found such an action impossible even to contemplate, not to mention the confusion of actors who would not know which one to—and so forth—

The interpreter struggled with my faltering efforts. As I knew, the production manager understood perfectly what I was getting at. He cut across faltering and interpreting. He banged his fat knees with his big handsome hands. He roared at us and in English! "American director must be strong! American director must say to everybody, 'You are listening to me!'"

He beat his barrel chest to illustrate how the American director must behave. The American, however, was unmoved. He said with frightful calm, "I know how to behave like this in my own country. I will not behave like this in Japan. I must ask that the Japanese director be removed."

The two men stared, not to say glared, at each other. I opened my handbag and took out the Chinese fan I keep for such emergencies. Although the room was well cooled, I found it necessary to fan myself. I tried to think about something remote and pleasant, the mountains of Vermont, for example, as seen from my living room window there.

I heard a loud gust of a sigh. It was the production manager. He got up and stalked about the room, rubbing his head with his hands. He was muttering, still in English. "I am fearing something like this to happen—oh yes, goddam!"

He sat down and pondered. I know my Japan and I understood that he was very unhappy. Somebody had to lose face, and it could not be the aged and famous Japanese director. Nor could it be ourselves, since as foreigners, we do not know enough to lose face. He lifted his head and sent me a reproachful look. You, he conveyed to me, you know better. You should have spared me this.

"I am sorry," I murmured from behind my fan. "I am so very sorry. But what can I do? If I had not told you, if we had gone on location, trouble would have been worse."

"Ah, sodeska," he sighed. "True—better get it over."

He relapsed into Japanese. He could not speak English any more. "Tell them," he said to the interpreter, "tell them that I will attend to it. Tomorrow I will see them. I am busy but I will see them." He turned his back as soon as possible, and we returned to the hotel.

"At least it's done," I told the American.

He refused to be cheerful. "We have not seen the end of it," he said grimly.

Next day it appeared that he was right. We returned to the studios and resumed casting. Everything was as it was the day before except we did not see the production manager, upon whom we depended for everything. Pretty actresses came in, reported that they had studied English for six years, declared that they could not speak English and left us again. Handsome young men came in with ditto. We were enormously cheered by an older actor who could take the part of Toru's father and spoke perfect English. And all this time there was no production manager. When we inquired of a pretty girl, she went away and returned to say that he could meet us in the city offices at two o'clock. He was very busy, et cetera. We were served delicious meat sandwiches—yesterday beef and today spiced pork. I pause here to say that the beef in Japan is made of beer-drinking Kobe cows, hand-massaged every day by devoted cowboys, and is tender beyond any beef I have ever tasted.

At two o'clock promptly we were in the city offices. No production manager appeared on the horizon of today or any day. The American became indignant and I became resigned. The pretty girls trotted off and returned to say that the production manager would see us at five o'clock the next day, or the next or the next. This meant a delay in deciding upon our cast which we simply could not afford. We went back to the hotel and complained to my special friend by telephone. It was useless to think of food or sleep if the production manager had abandoned us. There was a long wait. She called us. This time the American took the brunt. He explained his position, unaltered and unalterable. He listened to her reply and his face cleared for the first time in two days. I gathered that the matter of the Japanese director had been settled. He had been invited to resign. Everything would be all right, my friend said.

But late at my solitary dinner I found myself suddenly without appetite, although a delicious crabmeat salad was put before me. A horrid knowledge stirred in me, an echo of the past, my past in Asia. Everything was not all right—not quite, not quite. There is always a price for victory. What it would be I did not know. I still do not know. A debt remains unpaid. I can only hope the production manager will not—what? It is quite possible I shall never know. At any rate, the episode was over for the day.

And always at the end of the day, every day, there came the return to no one! After the problems, solved and unsolved, after the coming and going of many people, the doubt and concern, the excitement of discovery, the shared laughter, the growing confidence in the work, each day had the same end. I went back to my hotel rooms, unlocked the door, went in and locked the door again. Flowers were fresh, the rooms cool, letters heaped on the table—letters from no one. The one letter I longed for could never be written because he was gone. I did not open the others. Let them wait until my Japanese secretary came and I was forced to work in order that she could work. Invitations were many, but I had no enjoyment in accepting them. A few I must accept, those which had to do with the sad and anxious parents of retarded children, a few others from old friends for the sake of past kindness. I fell then into the habit of having dinner sent to my rooms and of eating alone, so that I need not be compelled to smile at strangers who might approach me with questions and praise. When night came, life was suddenly meaningless.

Yet I was not impatient with myself. I knew from experience that time is needed for the absorption of sorrow into one's being. Once that adjustment is made, growth begins again and new life. It was too soon. I found it was impossible to sit alone in the hotel rooms. Had he been with me, it would have been the best part of the day. It always was the best part. Much of our life had to be spent in separation during the hours of day, for each of us had a profession, a work. But how eagerly we looked forward to the evening, and to what lengths we went in order to spend it together! We went together wherever we had to go, I yielding to his necessity, he to mine, depending upon the importance we attached to the specific occasion. And in the twenty-five years of our married life we did not spend a night apart, until it became necessary for him to live and work entirely at home. Even then I refused all invitations that kept me away for a night, until he ceased to know whether I was there or not. And when he ceased to know, everything was different, except memory.

I have discarded that time of not knowing. When I think of him, I think of him as I knew him, vivid, alive, with infinite variety in thought and word, dominant, invincibly prejudiced in some matters, as I used to say impetuously when we disagreed, and he smiled and accepted the accusation with amusement and no intention of changing himself. But he knew I did not want him changed. Whatever he was, he was himself, and I liked that. For example, he could not drive a nail without pounding his thumb and therefore wisely he refused to drive nails. He took no part in household matters, however busy I was. He would not eat what he did not like, no matter how good the dish might be for him. At the same time he disciplined himself in amount and quality of what he did eat. When he spoke, none of us interrupted. He was the father as well as the husband, and yet he refused to have any part in disciplining our big family. I am no disciplinarian myself, being given to laughter over naughtiness unless I am angry, and neither mirth nor anger is the right atmosphere for discipline. Teachers of our nine children were unanimous in one comment, always made sooner or later to us, but particularly to me, for he would not attend parent-teacher meetings and I had to go alone. The comment was simple. "Your children are spoiled."

I agreed helplessly. How could it be otherwise when they had a mother who laughed too easily, and if she did not get angry easily, nevertheless when she did, she was in such vast temper that the child looked on astonished and thought she did not mean it? As for him, the extent of his discipline was to stare at the refractory child with cool disapproval and then turn to me with a remark made so casually that it stunned me unfailingly into feeble retort.

"Do you allow this sort of thing to go on?" he would ask.

"Do you?" I would ask.

Silence after that, and the child, isolated by our silence, usually subsided after a few minutes of trying to maintain independence. Looking at these same children now, I can only say that so far as I know, they have turned out well. That is, none of them is delinquent or has been in jail. Of course there is still time for jail but I doubt they will ever come to it.

Am I being quite fair to him as a disciplinarian? Perhaps not, for there was one offense which he would not tolerate from any child, and this was act or word which he considered a sign of lack of respect for me. If a child so behaved, his response was instant, invariable and thunderous.

"Don't you know your mother is the greatest person in the world?"

The absurdity of this remark wilted me at once into a state of embarrassment, which the children understood and suffered with me, especially as they never intended disrespect. I enjoyed free argument and spirited disagreement and his outburst killed communication. If we were at the table, our appetites failed and we sat in silence. What he thought of this silence I do not know, for he allowed no protest or discussion on the subject of respect for me, even from me, myself!

As for me, I obeyed him far too literally and this for two reasons. I had spent my life in China until we met, and I had been taught that woman should obey man, if possible. Second, I was disgracefully ignorant about my own country. I was born a late child and my parents had lived decades in China before I appeared in their life. They were young when they left home, my father twenty-eight and my mother only twenty-three, and both of them were idealists and intellectuals. They grew to maturity in Chinese culture and society and not in their own. When I came to live finally in my own country and we were married, he and I, he said that among other enjoyments it was fun to be married to me because I was so ignorant that he could tell me all the old American jokes and they were new to me. This was true, and he should have lived to tell them all, for he never got to the end. At any moment he would tell something that sent me into healthy laughter.

In only one family decision was he wrong, and I know now that I should have disobeyed him for practical reasons. Even at that he was right in principle. Here it is: he did not believe in homework for children. He contended, and rightly, that the school had the child all the best hours of the day. If the curriculum was carefully planned and all nonsense and waste of time eliminated, everything could be completed within school hours. He believed that family life in the evenings should not be destroyed by the child having to work on daytime school tasks. As usual, what he disapproved, he ignored. I had not been educated in the American school system, and knew no better than to agree with him. Consequently we all enjoyed our evenings together in music and games and reading aloud. The result showed, alas, in the children's report cards, and in a general attitude, I must confess, of considering school a pastime rather than work. I repeat, I should not have obeyed him. I should have gathered the children around the big table at night, and seen to it that they did their homework, until they were old enough to assume responsibility for themselves. . . . Yet what would have been his fate, in that case? Lonely evenings and no happy evening memories, and I am glad that we lived as we did.

In such half-smiling, half-tearful reminiscence I relapsed too easily and it was necessary to take myself in hand. So, when dinner was over, and the little Japanese waitress, always solicitous when I left my plate only half-empty, had removed the table, I sauntered again into the streets of Tokyo. I went often to the Ginza, market, bazaar and amusement place, always diverted by the variety of people who came to enjoy the gaudy scene. Flags, balloons, paper flowers of every color tied to the eaves of the roofs floated above the streets and shops; open to the street were exhibitors who demonstrated their many wares. American cars, a proof of wealth, stood waiting by the curbs, the chauffeurs zealously polishing the chromium while their employers explored toys or silks or jewelry. Bicycles dashed madly through the swarming crowds and women clattered along on wooden geta, their babies strapped to their backs.

Most significant of all were the young men and women who wandered hand in hand in a state of dazed happiness, window shopping, or just wandering. It takes getting used to, this hand-in-hand business in modern Japan. It is something entirely new. In old Japan lovers met in secret and climbed volcanoes and threw themselves into the fiery craters to signify the depth of their hopeless love. Nowadays they walk hand-in-hand in the Ginza or go on picnics to the famous spots where once they committed suicide together. Have the parents changed or is it the young who have learned to demand their rights? Certainly there is some change in the parents. The four chief catastrophes of old Japan, if we are to trust an ancient Japanese saying, were "earthquakes, fires, floods and fathers." Earthquakes, fires and flood are still to be feared, but fathers?

There is a change in fathers certainly, but the greatest change is in the mothers. No mother in old Japan would have dreamed of allowing her daughter to walk hand-in-hand with a young man in the Ginza or anywhere else, nor would the daughter have dreamed of disobedience. But I must take this change in the Japanese woman gradually and bit by bit. It is profound and overwhelming.

As for the Ginza, though the merchandise was astounding, garish, clamorous and sometimes beautiful, the people were my diversion—are my diversion wherever I wander. Thanks to them, I escape from myself. When midnight came and the crowd dispersed—for the Japanese go early to bed, except the gentlemen of the bars—I returned to my hotel rooms, let myself in again, locked the door, and went to bed.

In the strange floating existence of those days and nights, I went one evening to the Kabuki Theater by invitation of the star actor. The troupe had returned from a successful engagement in New York, but I had not gone to see them there. Somehow Kabuki seemed incongruous to me in that most modern of cities, and one time or another, perhaps, I would be in Tokyo again. The play that evening was the same one they had presented in New York, *The White Snake*. I knew the story well, for it is an ancient Chinese tale. The White Snake is a woman who assumes the form of a serpent for purposes of her own.

The night was clear and the streets of Tokyo were unusually crowded. I took a cab, and we arrived at the theater entrance, a vast place hung with paintings and filled with exhibits and crowded with people. Someone was waiting to meet me. The star had declared that he would not begin the show until he had met me and we had been photographed. I was led backstage and there he stood, made-up as a woman, the White Snake. It was a perfect make-up, sinister and graceful. He wore a close-fitting white kimono, without a trace of color. The headdress was white and his face, neck and hands were painted snow white. Even his lips were white, though lined at the inner edge with scarlet. The eyes were a snake's eyes, black and glittering, their glance darting here and there. When he saw me he put out his hand, and I took it and it felt cold and smooth in my hand. I wanted to put it down because it was cold and smooth as a snake's skin but it clung to mine, and thus, hand in hand, we were photographed. He talked for a few minutes, his stiff white lips scarcely moving, and then the gong struck and it was time for him to go on stage.

I went to my seat in the theater and there spent a few hours of pure pleasure. The stage was enormous, larger than any stage I had ever seen, and the spectacle superb. Amid masses of color and splendor, the White Snake moved with a sinuous composure, at once terrifying and symbolic, and I had never seen the play performed more powerfully and beautifully. There is no art in the world, in my opinion, which surpasses Kabuki in imaginative power. But perhaps this is partly because the stories of these plays have been a part of my childhood and I live through them again. At any rate the Japanese audience was absorbed as they can be only in this theater. When the play was over we walked out in a dream of silence.

The immense stage, the enormous cast, the splendor of the costumes and the extraordinary lighting made me realize again in contrast the cramped and narrow stage of Broadway. Year by year theater there has been compressed and diminished simply because of the cost of putting on a play. A great art is being strangled by craftsmen and mechanics in unions. Playwrights, directors and actors have offered a cut in their earnings but there is no such willingness on the part of the union workmen. I lingered after the play in the Kabuki Theater that evening and talked about it with Japanese friends over a bowl of tea. They had visited New York and they maintained that Japanese theater could never suffer such disaster. "We love art too well," they said. "We realize the spiritual and emotional benefits of art. Even our workmen realize this, and they would never destroy such an important part of our life merely for the sake of personal greed."

I hope they are right.

It was long past midnight when I reached my hotel rooms. When I was ready for bed, I went to the window as is my habit wherever I am in the world before I sleep, and looked out over the quiet city. An old moon hung crookedly in the sky, and its pale light shone down upon the roofs. At this moment, I felt again the deep inner quiver of an earthquake. It began as a tremor and then rose into a rolling motion. A picture fell, books slipped from the desk, a bowl of flowers crashed to the floor. I clung to the window sill and felt my heart pound against my ribs. Was this to be dangerous . . . ? No. . . . The earth grew still again. Only the moon hung there, unchanged and fixed. I waited a few minutes more, then put the books into place and filled the bowl with water for the flowers.

It was long before I could sleep. The earth tremor had somehow shaken the roots of my temporary world. I recognize the need in myself for roots. I suppose it is the result of my childhood in China. Well as I loved that country and must always so love it, nevertheless I was at the same time always aware of the turmoil over which we lived, the possibility that at any moment the angers and discontents existing for centuries against the western peoples might flame into crises in which we, innocent as we were individually, might lose our lives, as indeed we very nearly did and more than once. Perhaps this childhood remembrance of ever present uncertainty, over which I had no more control than a leaf in a storm, has always haunted me—or did until he came. Now that he was gone, the old subterranean awareness of danger returned again.

He had no such dark shadows. Resolutely cheerful, naturally gay, he never expected or suspected catastrophe. When compelled by the fact, he had an odd habit of deciding when he would face it. The method was simple but absolute. He marshaled all the blackest possibilities and wrote them down in his clear firm handwriting. Then he took from his desk his father's large gold watch and decided upon the day and the hour when he would attack the total problem. It was always at the last possible moment. Until it came, he was his usual charming self. He always found solution, or at least escape, and if the latter, it was not by any of the Chinese thirty-six ways. He never ran away.

I had come to depend very much on his genius for dealing with the improbable, for solving the insoluble and achieving the impossible and this always without the help of friends. He had friends beyond number, high and low, some of them among the wealthiest men in the world, others poor. The wealthy did not help him in the two financial crises of his life. He weathered his crises alone and triumphantly. The poor borrowed money from him without shame. To my indignation, distributed on rich and poor alike, he maintained a smiling indifference.

"They mean no harm," he would say.

I hated the earthquake. It roused old fears and old fears reminded me again that his unshakable good humor, his cheerful pessimism, his flashes of impatience, his affectionate cynicism toward mankind, above all his gay acceptance of life as he found it were now no more. The old uncertainty was with me again, and forever.

The most modern theater, by way of contrast to Kabuki, was more of a shock than even I could take. It came about in this manner. We went one day to the production manager with a list of our tentative characters. We entered his office, preceded by a pretty girl, and found him that morning businesslike and dignified. The jovial man about town had totally disappeared. He delayed a proper time to show how busy he was and perhaps how important, and we knew he was both busy and important and we sat waiting. Tea appeared but the production manager was still busy. Finally he joined us and we gave him our list of actors. He pointed immediately to two doubtful names. He could not speak English at all that morning, it seemed. The pretty girl interpreting, he said that he merely suggested, he was not directing—this with a bitter look at the American—but we should make better choices for the two leading men than we had done. We agreed promptly but reminded him that the man we wanted most had not been released to us by his firm. Hearing this, he got up, walked around, rubbed his head, groaned loudly several times and talked through three telephones at once. Nothing happened except no—no—no—from three directions. He attached a pretty girl to a fourth telephone, sat behind his desk, and twisted his hair in both hands and groaned again. Then he knocked himself on the head with clenched fists and turned to us, beaming. He had an idea. The final performance of Japanese rock-and-roll singers and musicians was taking place at that very instant in his own rock-and-roll theater. He would accompany us there, we could see all the best rock-and-roll young men and we could then take our choice. He would command any whom we chose to be our actors. They would listen to him. "I am big producer," he said loudly and now in English.

We agreed with alacrity, he plunged ahead, a behemoth but amiable, and we followed to be packed into cars and delivered at the theater. It was a huge place, and when I was led to a seat in a box, the last and only seat in the enormous theater and reserved, of course, for the production manager himself, I was simply stunned by what I saw. All the teen-agers in Japan were assembled there, or so it seemed, certainly thousands and thousands of them.

I sat and stared at stage and audience alike. This was indeed a Japan new to me, rock-and-roll, dancing girls and singing boys, American songs, western songs sung in English, and only a very few Japanese songs. The girls screamed just as they do in my own country, and they sounded just as silly. What is this affliction of the young, spreading from land to land? Thousands upon thousands of young Japanese—oh, very young—the performers are in their teens or barely out of them, and very young girls in skirts and blouses ran out from the audience to hang wreaths of paper flowers and paper streamers on their male favorites. Only one girl sang, a handsome girl of eighteen with an excellent voice.

"What do the parents think of this?" I asked the production manager.

"It disgusts them," he said, "but what can they do?"

What can they do indeed, here or anywhere!

Our business, however, was to find actors. After the grand finale we went downstairs into a small hot room and interviewed three or four young men viewed on the stage through opera glasses as possibilities. We were hopeful, for they sang in English so well that we were led to think they might speak English. Such was not the case. The only sentence they spoke well was the same one. "I cannot speak English," and they had each studied English six years in school. Then we found one bright exception, a gentle-faced boy who is called the Eddie Fisher of Japan. He spoke beautiful English. The explanation was that his mother was half-English and he had learned at home. We asked him to come the next morning for an audition.

While all this was going on, I observed a change in the production manager. He was softening. He saw our problem of the six-year English and he felt concern. He invited us to have dinner with him, and asked if we wanted to go where he always goes, or to some more elaborate place. We accepted with grateful surprise, saying that we wanted to go where he went. We climbed in cars, again pushing through oceans of young people waiting for their favorite singers to emerge from the stage door, and soon we drew up before a restaurant which was not like any I had seen before. Obviously it was not a tourist resort nor perhaps a place for women. I was not daunted, however, and the production manager evidently reigned here as everywhere. It was a fascinating place, small but clean as only Japanese know cleanliness, the rough wooden tables and counters made of six-inch-thick unpainted log slabs scrubbed to snow whiteness. The production manager gave orders in the manner of one always obeyed but he was obeyed, two slabs were put end to end and he assigned our seats. Mine faced him, and so I had full opportunity to observe this extraordinary man.

For now a new man appeared. He even announced that he was not the same man we had seen heretofore, and proceeded to explain himself and his life. He was not married, he told us, and he insisted that he was the loneliest man in Tokyo. He lived with his mother, a wonderful woman whom he adored, but he was fifty years old. He did not look that age. He looked a somewhat battered thirty-nine. Meanwhile he continued to tell us about his wretched life. All day long he went from one conference to another, preparing the weekly film picture he was compelled to produce. He woke early every morning in spite of late nights, and in the cold chill of dawn he read.

"What do you read?" I inquired with interest. Perhaps he read poetry or Zen Buddhism. He answered between clenched teeth.

"I read screen play only—hundred—hundred—hundred—pouring on me every day. . . . Always I am depressed afterward. So every night I am here, drinking."

The more he drank the better English he could speak. It was never perfect but it was expressive—and explosive. He did not cease also to speak Japanese. Indeed, he carried on an extraordinary bilingual monologue with the Japanese around us. He joked and when he saw that I was not drinking sakè he ordered a wine jug filled with water and then announced loudly that I was drinking outrageously and he bellowed laughter at his own wit. Suddenly he poured advice on the American director. A director, he said, cannot be a pure artist—not pure, not pure! He must have evil in him—outside nice, inside evil, evil, otherwise people will not be afraid of him. The American listened without reply, smiling. Suddenly the production manager struck his own head with clenched fists. He had an idea again, a glorious idea!

"Drinking, I am fountainhead for idea," he declared, enraptured with himself.

His idea concerned my friend's son-in-law, a young actor of promise. His wife was proficient in English and could be very useful to everybody. If we would place them in our cast, all feelings could be saved and all hearts assuaged. He reminded us that he had suffered much pain when he had to tell great Japanese director he was not to work on the film with us. He had to assume full responsibility himself for a sad mistake and he had to bow to the lowest level and this hurt. But he could forgive us if—

We replied that of course we would like to see the two young people but the picture must be considered before feelings. He was already on the telephone, however, and after an outburst in Japanese returned to us, all good cheer and satisfaction.

"Now," he exclaimed. "We must be happy. Bar or geisha house?"

We asked him to decide for us. "Bar, of course," he declared. "Geisha is too old-fashion. In bar, relaxation. Top class bar. I go every night there."

We took cabs again and rocked through crowded streets. Japanese taxi drivers are described in agitated detail by every American tourist, and I need not add to these descriptions except to say that everything said about them is true. They are zealously kind, emotionally involved with every passenger, and utterly careless about life, limb or property of anyone, including themselves.

The bar, as we entered, seemed to be a number of small comfortable rooms clustered around a bar. The production manager began relaxing immediately by loosening his belt and taking off his tie. The bar was small and crowded with business men and with pretty girls, of whom there were many. I was introduced to a slender handsome woman of young middle age, whom the production manager declared was best madame in Tokyo. She looked competent and modest and upon hearing my name fell into a state of emotion, declaring that she had read all my books. I had been her idol, et cetera. I was touched but slightly embarrassed. She introduced her girls to me after we were seated, very crowded, into a circular bench against the bar itself; these girls sat by me, one by one, and through one of them who spoke English, I became somewhat acquainted with them. Most of them were married and had children. No, they did not enjoy bar work, they said, but their husbands had poor jobs, or no jobs and this was easy work. I detected or imagined a certain patient sadness in their eyes and was reminded of a visit I made once in Paris, many years ago, to the Folies Bergère. I was humanly curious then as now, and after the show I left my escort and went backstage to get acquainted with the show girls. They too were not girls. They were women, most of them married, with home problems of deserting husbands, sick husbands, poverty, illness—and most of them were not young.

"Why such work?" I had inquired.

"At night the children are asleep and safe."

"It is better than leaving them all day," and so forth, the same in Paris as in Tokyo—

Our talk was now interrupted by the production manager. "My best friend," he announced, and presented a very small girl.

Her face was a cameo of sadness. I had already noticed her. She had been sitting beside a fatuous business man and serving him with liquor and condiments. Once, with my accursed, noticing, novelist's eye, I saw him put his arm around her too closely and she shrank away with a look in her eyes that for pity's sake I will not describe. She sat beside me now, saying nothing, just looking at me with such deep quiet that I felt communication. Of this I do not speak.

The night wore on. I rose to leave. The madame, whom the girls call "mama," assembled a line to bow farewell. She herself came with me to the car and leaned in the window to talk, speaking English rather well. She had had an education and was not a shallow or silly woman. She kept looking at me with warmth and affection, pressed my hands, gave me a great bouquet, and let me go reluctantly.

Alone in the car I pondered upon this phenomenon of Japanese life, the night life of men apart from their families. It is a force destructive to family life, a relic of feudalism. The modern Japanese woman hates the bars and geisha houses which take their men away from home. Old-fashioned Japanese women accepted them as they accepted anything men did, but modern Japanese women long for real companionship with the men they love. Yet men still continue to stay away from home, "and I have learned," as my little Japanese secretary said one day with a cold calm, "to nag him no more. I have even learned how to greet him with a happy smile at two o'clock in the morning."

Yes, she could do it. The Japanese woman has always been stronger than the Japanese man, for, like the Chinese woman, she has been given no favors. She has never heard of chivalry or knights in golden armor. She was born a female—that is to say, an inferior person, a bearer of burdens, an obedient slave. In centuries of such existence, while she compelled herself to devotion and duty, she accumulated an inner strength which cannot be surpassed. She gave birth to man, tended him and cared for him, shielded and defended him without question. Why should she question when there was none to answer? She was betrayed by only one person, another kind of woman, the woman who did not marry, the woman who was not bowed down with household cares and children, the woman taught and trained and groomed to amuse men. She was betrayed by geisha. All that a man could not find in his uneducated houseworn wife, whom he needed, nevertheless, for comfort and household ease, he sought and found in the geisha, whose only duty was to please him, to attract his eye, to entice him with music, to win his mind by her education. The best geisha is a brilliant and intelligent woman. She has her counterpart in the Greek hetaira, against whom Greek wives also wailed their accusations.

I inquired one day of a beautiful geisha, "Do you feel no concern for the wife of this man whom you have captured?"

She shrugged her shoulders. "It is the men who create the demand. We are merely merchandise."

A cynical reply, and her modern counterpart, the bar girl, is in every way her inferior. A well-trained geisha could be, in her own fashion, a woman of distinction and grace. Any woman, it seems, can be a bar girl. If her face is half pretty, she is lucky, but if it is not very pretty, she has other wares to sell. Her influence on men is even less fortunate than that of the geisha. She is less graceful, less distinguished in every way. She is sometimes no more than a dead-end kid and is nearly always a prostitute. Geisha can be prostitutes but are not compelled to be. They may keep their hold on men in other ways, if they so desire. The bar girl has few resources beyond her sex, and at this moment sex is more crude than ever before in Japan. Naturalism there has always been, but sex, *per se,* is used by women now as a lure and a weapon, and by men as an escape, comparable to alcoholism. Escape from what? Desperation and a sense of personal inferiority, I suppose. What else does the human male seek to escape?

Geisha and bar girls aside, however, something has happened to young Japanese women, and I rather imagine that the something is American men. Many Japanese women have been courted by American men, and the two, man and woman, have been surprised to find what each had been seeking for a long time—the woman, a man who appreciates gentleness and deference and a naturalistic attitude toward sex; the man, a woman who has been taught to defer to him, and to serve him, to believe that his sexual interest in her is all the love she should expect from any man. Although I do remember a certain young American man who complained that a Japanese woman made a wonderful wife when she first came to America, but after two years she was no better than an American, having learned American female ways!

Be that as it may, young women in Japan have not learned

American ways. They are liberated, that is all. They move everywhere with delightful freedom and composure, at once daring and feminine, bold and shy, an enchanting combination of apparent innocence and actual sophistication which, if not permanent, is very attractive while it lasts. And perhaps if she lives in America, she may discover that the young American man is often a charming but perpetual boy, and what pleased and surprised her at first palls when the boy does not grow up. I know a certain American who brought a beautiful young Japanese wife home with him and introduced her with enthusiasm to his welcoming parents. A year later this same young woman announced that she wished to have a divorce because she had fallen in love with another man. The man, it appeared, was his own father, who had also fallen in love with her. The older man wanted an adoring wife, and the Japanese wife had been trained to adore, and the young woman wanted, as she said, "a more wise man."

Perhaps there are no rules for this eternal game between man and woman. The Japanese man, so far as I could see, has not changed very much. I wonder if he will like his woman when he discovers what she really is. As yet he does not know.

That night when I went to my hotel room, full of such thoughts, it was raining, the streets were deluged with flood waters and the rain thundering down enclosed me in a box of sound. I am claustrophobic and I escaped through the silent corridors of the vast new part of the hotel, where my rooms were, to the old building put up by Frank Lloyd Wright. It was one of his early manifestations, and certainly it does not in the least resemble his later work, the Guggenheim Museum in New York or the Dallas Little Theater. Nor does it resemble anything in Japan. It is a curious heap of tessellated edges and corners and over-decoration. Its glory is that it has stood through all earthquakes and this because the architect discovered that Tokyo itself was built on a quivering sea of mud. Into this sea he sank thousands of Oregon pine logs and on that foundation built his monstrosity. It actually floats and can therefore adjust to anything.

Does floating lead to adjustment? I pondered upon the question as I sought one of the many corners in the dark old lobby. If so, then I must be adjusting. It seemed to me that I was not living, not even existing, only floating upon the surface of time. To rise in the morning and work, to walk alone at night, to sleep briefly and get up at dawn, not thinking of past or of future, but only of this one day, this one night, and pondering on men and women, I was reminded how rare an experience of marriage mine had been. I am not an easy-to-marry woman, or so I imagine. I am divided to the bottom of my being, part of me being woman, the other part artist and having nothing to do with woman. As an artist I am capable of cruelty, for artists are ruthless and must be.

"Can you bear it," I once asked him, "if you see yourself in a novel? Not just as you are, of course—I always create my own people, but I steal whatever I need—the ways in which you asked me to marry you, for example, which I am sure no man ever used before. I might need a few of them sometime for other men and women."

He smiled. He had a wonderful smile, beginning in his deep blue eyes—eyes wasted on a man, for they were pure violet with long black lashes, but I liked them, and so perhaps they were not wasted. "Take it," he said. "It's yours anyway. Take anything I have to give—"

The unique attribute he had was that he understood an artist. I doubt he understood women or cared to understand them. He had a low opinion of women in general. He did not dislike them but his attitude was impersonal and somewhat condescending. When I complained that he was unjust he replied calmly,

"I don't look down on women at all. On the contrary, I think they could be much more than they are. They rate themselves too low if they are content to be cooks, cleaning women, and nursemaids when they can be anything they wish to be and do whatever they like. Nobody stops them except themselves."

Since he himself had an English gentleman's attitude toward housework—he was English on both sides and his mother was born in England—I felt a pervading injustice in these remarks, but I am not one to carry on an argument and certainly he was no puritan, so far as women were concerned. He began life early, graduating from Harvard as an honors man when he was only twenty and marrying at once. He was attractive to women and knew it, with blue eyes and black hair and brown skin. His manners were charming, deceptively so sometimes when he was talking with a woman. Yet he had his own invincible code. He would not, for example, call a woman in his employ by her first name or invite her to luncheon or arrange a meeting with her outside of office hours. He felt that any demand of a personal nature made upon an employee was unfair use of employer's power. I remember that he had at one time a secretary who was an unusually young and pretty girl. When a male friend or business caller made teasingly envious remarks he was cold as only an Englishman can be.

"Miss Kirke is an efficient secretary or I would not employ her," was his invariable reply.

The result of such an attiude was, of course, the total devotion of his secretaries. Even today, when Miss Kirke is married and has grown children, she and the others like her say to me in loving remembrance,

"He was so much fun to work for—and you could trust him. He never made passes at you. You could be yourself."

A humble tribute, but how significant! And yet he could make me happily furious sometimes. For example, he liked to say that I was unlike any other woman he had ever known because, he said, I had the brain of a man in the body of a woman. I flew out at him, invariably, at such a notion. Why should a woman, I demanded, be said to have the brain of a man merely because she had a good mind? Did Nature give the supreme gift only to men? Was there a law of inheritance which denied brains to women? He laughed, pretended to seek shelter, and then said gravely that I was right.

"I apologize," he said, his eyes twinkling, but of course he never apologized for what he believed.

What was precious beyond diamonds to me was the fact, indisputable, that he enjoyed my mind. He liked profound conversation on abstruse subjects. He enjoyed repartee. And far beyond diamonds and life itself was the fact that he understood I had to be alone when I was writing. He never asked what I was writing or even what the book was about. When a novel was finished and typed and ready to be given to the publisher I took it to him myself and presented it formally, Chinese fashion, with both hands. His office was next to mine, but there were two doors between. His was the older building, and the short passageway was once the smoke house, where farmers for a hundred years smoked ham and bacon. The two doors were always closed when I was writing and he never opened them, but he rose when I came in with the finished work and received it gravely.

"This is a big day," he always said.

A big day it always was, and he put aside everything else and sat down to the task he loved, he told me, above all others, the reading of a manuscript I had written. He edited carefully but sparely. I do not remember that he ever made a change involving anything more serious than a misplaced preposition or a time confusion. The Chinese language has few prepositions and I have never quite learned to manage these refractory and precise little English words. As for time confusion, it was something from which I had always to be saved. I have no sense of time. I do not mean that I am unpunctual. On the contrary, I learned early to be punctual to a fault—I say to a fault for I am too punctual and waste my own time waiting for other people. My parents were two separately busy persons who lived on separate schedules into which I as a child had to fit. I live on schedule, too, as a separately busy person and so did he. No, I mean that I pay no heed to what year it is, what month, or what day. I cannot remember birthdays, anniversaries, or any of the important dates women are supposed to remember. A secretary has to remember for me and warn me in advance. He, on the other hand, had the disconcerting habit of perfect time recall. On any morning at the breakfast table, or at any time during the day, he could look at his watch and ask,

"Do you remember what we were doing ten–twenty–(etc.) years ago at this moment?"

At first, wanting to be perfect, I tried to remember. Later, resigned to myself, I said boldly that I did not remember. Then he would tell me.

"It was the first time I kissed you–or proposed to you–or you said you wouldn't have me–or I took you by surprise in Yokohama, etc., etc."

The chase had indeed been a long one. We were past our first youth when we first met, each resigned, we thought, to unsatisfactory marriages, and each well-known in our own fields. I had firmly refused him in New York, Stockholm, London, Paris, and Venice, and then had sailed by way of India for home in Nanking, China.

In six months he cabled me to meet him in Shanghai in order to hear "no" again and this time forever. I went alone after that to Peking for some months of research necessary for the completion of my translation of *Shui Hu Chuan* or *All Men Are Brothers*, and had been there less than a week when he appeared unexpectedly in the midst of a violent dust storm out of the Gobi desert. We parted again eternally and he went to Manchuria and I home again to Nanking to pack my bags for a summer visit to the United States to see that all was well there with my retarded child. I had my younger daughter and my secretary with me, and was in a resigned state of mind when I left, so far as he was concerned. I had, I thought, made the wise decision. I did not want turmoil in my life.

It was a fine July morning, I remember, and we were docking at the pier in Yokohama. I had planned not to go ashore, for I had been many times in the city. Instead I would work on my translation and my secretary would take my little girl to the park. I had no sooner settled myself to my lonely task when I heard the voice which was now the one I knew best in all the world.

"I've turned up again—I shall keep on turning up, you know—everywhere in the world. You can't escape me."

There he was, lean, brown, and handsome, and smoking his old briar pipe. . . . In spite of that, I said "no" every day on board ship and again in Vancouver and all winter in New York. But spring in that magic city was my undoing and we were married on the eleventh of June and lived happily ever after, together as man and wife, separately in our professional work.

He was a great editor—I have seen him take a muddle of a manuscript and make it a unified whole—but he would have been a fine critic. He would have judged the writer on how well he had accomplished the goal he had set for himself, and not have befuddled the reader by irrelevant remarks of his own. And he was a genius of his own sort in coaxing books out of writers who did not know they were writers. A notable example was a short manuscript that came to him one day from an American woman in Siam. He was then editor and owner of *Asia* magazine. I remember the article. It was entitled "The King's English," and the King was the King of Siam. The author had done a nice little piece of research into the King's vernacular English, which was fearful and delightful. But he saw much more than the light little essay. He saw a character and a man, and he invited the American woman to write more about this King. A few articles arrived and at last, upon his persuasion and encouragement, a book-length manuscript. He set to work to create a book out of the material he found there and to demand what was not there. The result eventually was a fascinating book, which he called *Anna and the King of Siam*, and this book later became a fabulous musical on Broadway, *The King and I*, by Rodgers and Hammerstein.

The list is distinguished. He was the one who brought Jawaharlal Nehru's great books to Americans, and through his publishing company to readers all over the world. He was the one who discerned in the young Sukarno of Indonesia the promise of a future Asian leader and encouraged him to write his first book and so become known to the West. He was the one who published the first book in the

United States of warning against Nazism, a prophecy so far ahead of its time, though not of reality, that it found few readers. And he was the one, too, who edited all of Lin Yutang's best books and first established his reputation as a writer. He had the gift of a universal comprehension, an eclectic mind, a synthesizing judgment, enlivened by faith in talent wherever he found it.

He was proud of being a publisher and he felt it a noble profession. Making money was never his impetus. If a book was good enough to merit publishing, he accepted it with enthusiasm, and this whether or not he agreed with what it said. His own opinions were always firmly on the side of the intelligent liberal. In a strongly Republican family he voted for the Democrats, occasionally varying it for the Socialists as a protest vote. Yet he published authors who were conservative and sometimes in the narrowest sense. He believed that they too had a right to be heard and if they presented their opinions well, he gave their books the same editorial care he gave to all others. The range of the authors he developed was from Fritz Sternberg to James Burnham.

An editor, he believed, had the high privilege of discovering talent and the duty of helping it to develop to its best fruit and then of presenting it to the world. He was an impresario of writers and books, but a man of such tender understanding of the needs and delicacies and shynesses of talented persons, that he guided without seeming to do so, drawing forth their ideas by skillful questions and honest praise and appreciation. Of the numerous letters I received after his death many were from writers who said that until he helped them to understand themselves they had not been able to write.

And of myself what shall I say? It was he who saw something in my first small book, a tentative effort rejected by all other publishers until he perceived in it the possibility that its author might one day write a better book. His staff was equally divided against the book, and it fell to him as the president of the company to cast his vote. He voted for it, and on that narrow chance my life began.

Ah me, it does not do to dream too long. The lobby of

the old Imperial Hotel in Tokyo was empty except for a sleepy clerk. The rain had stopped and a new moon was swinging above the clouds when I walked outside to breathe the cooled night air. The new moon? I had been in Tokyo for three weeks. For two months I had been alone.

Music has always been an important part of my life, background and medium for thought and feeling. For the picture I wanted Japanese music, not the synthetic nonsense that passes for Oriental in our American attempts, but original creation in Japan and by a Japanese. Moreover, it must be modern Japanese, for the change that has taken place in every aspect of Japanese life is nowhere more evident than in music. Music is the barometer—and thermometer, for that matter—of every culture, the art most revelatory of a people's temperament, character and response to outer influence. I was pleased, then, when Toshiro Miyazumi said that he would like to write the music for *The Big Wave.* I knew his work, but I had never met him and it was a special pleasure to find him waiting for me one morning in my hotel sitting room. He rose and introduced himself and at the same time handed me a gift, a record of his symphony, *Nirvana.*

"I am your composer," he said modestly.

We sat down and I looked at his face frankly. It was a charming face, strong and gentle, quiet and poetic and without guile. An innocent face, I would have said, except that it was not the face of a child, although there was a child's openness in the expression. I recognized this quality, for it is to be found only in highly gifted persons, wise as serpents and gentle as doves, as the old book puts it.

"I am fortunate," I told him.

Toshiro Miyazumi is called the Leonard Bernstein of Japan and he does indeed resemble Bernstein in the brilliance of his talent. Unlike Bernstein, however, he devotes himself to composing music. True, he has conducted, but he prefers to compose.

"Please tell me about yourself," I said.

There was nothing to tell, it seemed. He bit his lip, he tried to remember.

"You were born in 1929," I reminded him.

A flash of gratitude lighted his charming calm face. "Ah yes, I was born but I began my life at six years of age, composing and playing the piano."

"Then?"

He considered and finally spoke. "I went to the University of Tokyo."

I was about to inquire, "Nothing between?" and decided not to speak. I would wait and let him present his life as he saw it. There was nothing, then, between six and the University of Tokyo.

He continued after reflection.

"When I was twenty-one I received a scholarship to Paris for one year, to the Conservatoire. There was a man, Tony Oben, teaching me. Very conservative, not interested in the new method of composing . . . So I was a bad pupil. Because the techniques there were formal, the rhythms old-fashioned somewhat and harmony traditional. . . . Creation is different. The energy is emotion. I cannot, because I use the twelve tone method. So I searched and went to Austrian composers—Arnold Schoenberg, Anton Webern, who use new methods to express contemporary composition."

"But you use classical themes, too," I reminded him. "You are versatile—"

He accepted this with a smile. "It is very difficult to support my life on classical music alone, however I love it. I returned to Japan and for several years composed many kinds of music, orchestral, chamber, and so forth, as well as for musical films. I suppose television and radio music were my job, but I want always to be an artist. . . ."

There was a long pause, covering years. "So after five years I went back to Europe, and I went to music festivals in Sweden and Germany and other places where my music was played."

"How does it feel to hear your music played across the world?" I asked.

He gave me an eloquent look and was too modest for words. "I came back to Japan and I made a group for contemporary music and some prizes were given to me. That is all."

All is a good deal for a young man of thirty-one, but apparently his story was told. He was not in the least shy, and he sat relaxed and waiting.

"And this record?" I asked, indicating the gift.

"It was played in Tokyo, première in April, second day, 1958, after working about a year."

"Are you interested in religion? The title suggests Buddhism."

"The Japanese Buddhist temple bell," he said. "It is a typical mixture of sounds. I am very fond of it, since I am interested in concrete music and electronic music, that is, creating musical structures out of sound energy, as Edward Varese suggests. In other words, the method of composition is by giving musical life to the energy inherent in the sound itself. So I bring new timbres into my compositions—for example, mixed tones. Combinations of several dozen pure tones have become dominant in my works."

The calm face had suddenly become animated and beautiful.

"I am attracted by the voices of Buddhist priests chanting sutras—no melody, of course, but habitual intonation and rhythm, and when any priests take part together, the group produces a sort of musical noise through the mixing of the voices of varying pitches. I added to a full orchestra treble woodwind instruments and bass brass instruments, placed in different corners of the hall to achieve a directional sense by means of the crisscross of sounds over the heads of the audience—"

No silence now—the words poured from him in a flow of creating thought!

"Nirvana, the ideal state of being for the Buddhist, is symbolized by the toll of the bell. So perhaps I am religious. I composed this symphony with the idea of creating my own musical Nirvana. It is not religious music, I suppose, in the purest sense of the word. It is a sort of Buddhistic cantata. I hope you like it." He smiled suddenly. "I talk too much."

I broke the next silence. "What do you do next, after our picture?"

"I go to New York, to write music for the New York City Ballet. It will be played next season."

"Quite different from a Buddhist cantata?"

"I like difference, but before I go to New York I will finish the music for *The Big Wave*. This picture is unusual, too, and altogether different. I have the music in my mind clearly, really romantic, not Wagnerian romantic, strong and delicate together, with contemporary Oriental philosophy. How is it you write like this? The emotion is Oriental."

It was my turn not to know what to say. How can a writer say how she writes? But he had forgotten his question.

"I want a song in it," he was saying. "I want a song that is like the sunrise, young and fresh and full of hope. Your young people, beginning their life again in their own time, at this moment, never before lived, I want that song."

He leaned toward me, all demand and pleading. "If I write the music, will you write the words?"

"I cannot," I told him.

There was nothing more to be said. We shook hands and he was gone. And the song was written by someone else.

He stopped at the office the next day at noon and looked in. Something was always going on there, and that moment was no exception. Hundreds of costumes were heaped on the floor, and several persons—men, boys and a girl or two—were pawing them over to a running accompaniment of Japanese at various tonal levels. They were looking for some garment demanded by the model for various parts in the picture. The model was a microscopic human being, male, of vague age but certainly not young. He stood something under five feet and if he weighed ninety pounds, it would surprise me. He was skin and bone, and if the skeleton was a child's, the face was fascinating. Wrinkled, lively, full of fun and mischief, it was the face of an old faun. The top of the head was bald, but hair surrounded the large bald spot and stood straight out from the skull, as though the old faun were undergoing electric shock. He was certainly full of some sort of electricity for he was issuing orders without let, as he modeled a fisherman's outfit made for a man four times his size. He was a good model, nevertheless. He clutched the trousers in at his waist, gave a twist to the belt, arranged the Japanese coat and became a fisherman. Everybody laughed and I sat down to watch.

He knew all the characters in *The Big Wave*, it appeared, and he modeled them all. When he modeled a man he faced us. When he modeled a woman, he turned his back. I recognized each character, even the young girl Setsu. How an old man could pose so that he suggested a gay young girl, even from the back, is something I cannot explain. I wished for the millionth time that I understood Japanese, for whatever the old faun was saying the audience was convulsed. Every now and again he was dissatisfied and threw off a costume, or rejected what was offered and pawed among the confusion of the piled garments with all the fierce intensity of a monkey looking for fleas.

At this moment someone had an inspiration. "He's what we've been looking for—a wonderful attendant for Old Gentleman. Does he speak English?"

The old faun smiled with all his teeth, none of them in good repair, and shook his head to the English.

To the rest he replied that he would think it over and let us know tomorrow. The next day, the old faun, modeling more costumes, and dancing about on his spindly legs, brightened as I entered the room. A stream of Japanese flowed from him, which, interpreted, was that he would join the cast, but only if we promised not to cut his hair. He said he would not come with us if we cut his hair.

I regarded the circle of electrified black wire surrounding the bony bald skull. "Tell him," I said, "that I would not think of cutting that hair. I promise it will not be cut."

We all stared gravely at the valuable hair.

"Hai," the cheerful faun said with a smile that reached across the room. Suddenly the smile disappeared. Japanese chatter poured from where the smile was.

The patient interpreter explained. "He says, does he have to speak English? If so, he can't."

"He has only two lines and we will teach him every day," we promised.

More Japanese and the interpreter reported. "He says he must have a good teacher. He must speak English perfectly."

"He will have a good teacher," we promised.

Later we found that no amount of teaching could prevail over his invincible Japanese accent. We cut his lines to two essential words, "yes," and "no." These he says in the picture, impressively and with pride. He had, he said, waited his whole life to become an actor, but the nearest approach had been to work with costumes. I shall never forget his beatific face when he knew he was to have the part. So far as he was concerned, he was a star. He gave us a great smile and the faun became monkey again, pawing among the clothes, but now he was searching feverishly for his own costume.

That night for the first time since he left, I felt a release, slight though it was, from the dull oppression of—what shall I call it? Shock, desolation, loneliness, whatever its compound, it had laid a burden upon me from which I could not escape. I did not wander the streets that night. Instead I decided upon a Japanese massage, dinner alone in my room, a long letter to the children at home, and a book. This is a program ordinary enough, but I had not achieved it since being alone. Laughter had provided the possibility now. I laugh easily, since the world is full of funny people and incidents, but I had not laughed often in the past months and never without the self-forgetfulness that somehow the little faun had inspired that afternoon. It is the peculiar talent of the artist that he is able to enter the being of another person and this is particularly true of the novelist. We had discussed it often, he and I, and he had forgiven me always when, temporarily, I was absorbed in someone other than himself. It is a strange absorption this, and I do not know how to describe it except to liken it to the focus of total interest essential to the scientist theoretician. Such a scientist is by temperament an artist too and none of us can escape what we ourselves are.

I had not been able to absorb myself in anyone, however, since his death and until this afternoon when for an hour the old habit returned. I felt elated and almost hopeful. At least I was relieved, however briefly, of the miasma of sadness in which I had walked for so many weeks. I laughed with all my heart and for an hour was healed. I can report that I carried through my program for the evening and went to bed at a reasonable hour, also for the first time in all the weeks. The fact marked a beginning.

The abalone diving girls—have I spoken of them? I think not and I must, for they were a unique tightly knit little group in our all-Japanese cast. Abalone clams are a delicacy in the Japanese cuisine but they are difficult to obtain for they cling to rocks with a powerful muscle and they live far down where the sea is dark and the water icy cold. Japanese fishermen prudently refuse to dive for them and allot the task to young women, who are more able to endure the cold and the danger. Men row the boats to the clam beds and wait patiently while the women plunge into the sea, clad only in shorts and belts into which they thrust the long heavy iron knives necessary for hacking the clams from the rocks.

To my amazement, their costume, so natural to them and so sensible, became a matter of concern and even controversy with our American producers. American audiences, it seemed, could not tolerate the sight of the bare breasts of the women divers. In Europe the sight would be quite acceptable, even pleasant, but decency has absolute standards in the breast-conscious United States.

"How?" I inquired. "A woman is a woman and she cannot properly be anything else."

"Bras," the American delegate said laconically. He relented slightly when he saw my amazement. "We'll take two shots of them, one with and one without."

That is what we did, and I was amused to see how embarrassed the women were when compelled to wear pink brassieres over their round brown breasts. They felt really naked, as Eve did in the garden, doubtless, when she was told to wear a fig leaf.

A peculiar satisfaction in translating my story from one medium to another, from printed page to film, was that the characters came alive in flesh and blood. We found Setsu one day and I shall never forget the moment of pure angelic pleasure when, looking at a young woman, I recognized her. She was a young star of his own company, the production manager told us. More important to me was her lovely little face and large melting eyes of soft brown. She was so small in stature that she was, she told me, a member of the Transistor Club, whose members must all be under five feet. This transistor girl, however, was even smaller. When she stood by our six-foot, grown-up Toru in the film it was exactly right as he looked down upon her, laughed and said, "I like you because you are so small and funny."

Our cast was complete at last. They could all speak English or could learn the few words they must speak—except Toru's mother. She was simply too shy to attempt an English word. But she had so sweet a face, besides being a well-known actress in Japan, that we cut her lines and let her act instead of speak. Meanwhile three weeks had passed. All contracts were signed. It was a fine cast, Sessue Hayakawa the star best known in the western world. All the others were stars in Japan, except grown-up Haruko, a new actress chosen especially for the ferocious abalone diving girl, who fell in love with Toru and fought for him against gentle Setsu.

When we were ready to leave Tokyo at last, the cast assembled, the camera and crew waiting, Old Gentleman invited us to a party at a geisha house, and thither we went one evening, he having called for us in state to take us there in his own car. I had grown used by now to evenings spent in quiet inns with Japanese friends. A good inn, in Japan, is never to be found beside a highway. One must descend from car or bus and walk for at least a hundred yards, and likely more, down a mossy path to a secluded spot, where under trees, if possible, low roofs spread over rooms open to gardens and small pools. To such places, as often as I had felt inclined, friends had invited me, professors in universities, writers, playwrights, literary people and artists, groups of talented women.

Such evenings passed in restful conversation, comparisons in customs, and memories of peace and war and peace again. I enjoyed beyond expression the new freedom with which we could talk. Some barrier seemed to have rolled away in the years in which I had been absent from Japan, not from me but from them. I can only attribute it, at least in part, to the experience they have had with Americans during the years of Occupation and after. There had been misunderstandings, but understanding had prevailed.

The evening at the geisha house was not like the quiet evenings among congenial friends. We stopped at a sumptuous new restaurant and then entered a huge room where the longest low table I had ever seen was already surrounded by guests, all of whom, our host assured us, were the highest of their class. Thus we were introduced to an aged prince surrounded by geisha girls, of whom there were plenty, then to a minister of the present cabinet, then to a young giant seven feet tall and three feet wide, who was the champion wrestler in Japan, and so on and on. Each male guest had several geisha surrounding him, and even I was given two to attend me, right and left.

Between dishes, we were entertained by the traditional dancing and singing of trained geisha. What was new, however, were two young girls, magicians. They were among the best I have ever seen, and I have seen magicians in every country because I adore them. These girls, in contrast to the geisha, were in western dress, their arms bare to their shoulders. There was no nonsense therefore of hiding rabbits and fowl and pots of water up their sleeves. They simply did marvelous tricks and I have no idea how.

After some four enjoyable hours the evening came to an end. Reflecting upon its incidents, a bit of fluff sticks in my mind. The American Ambassador's wife had described to me, at a luncheon in my honor, the formal dresses still required of foreigners attending any function at the court or palace of the Emperor. The dresses, she told me, must be long and must have high necks and long sleeves. Later in the day I asked a Japanese friend of literal mind why foreign women must wear high necks. She answered promptly and exactly. "It is so when they bow the Emperor must not be embarrassed to look down their naked bosoms."

Our last night in Tokyo, the geisha party over, I sat by my window in the dark before I slept and looked out over the brilliant city, a mass of glittering modern buildings, in the center of which is the high and ancient wall surrounding the imperial palace. Yes, there is a moat. In the division of old and new, which is today's Japan, I am reminded of a courtesy call I had made that morning to the president of another great Japanese film company. He had been kind enough to lend to us one of his young stars to be our grown-up Toru.

In his way, this executive was remarkable, too. He is a small man, slender and healthy and full of energy. He has keen eyes and a brisk manner. I expressed my gratitude, and he said he wanted the picture to be a success. At this moment I observed high on the wall a miniature Buddhist temple. He is an ardent Buddhist, as I knew, and we talked for a few minutes about that great and ancient religion. I remembered that my scholar father once wrote a long monograph upon the subject of Buddhism as a source for certain Christian beliefs. There were more than thirty such resemblances and I told the distinguished Japanese Buddhist about them. He was deeply impressed, and said my father was entirely right—there is much in common between the two religions, and this not by accident, he was convinced, but by shared experience in history.

The next day, our very last, we obeyed Japanese custom by giving a party for cast and crew before we set out on great adventure. The big room we had rented from the hotel was crowded. All our actors were there, our cameraman—of him much more, for assuredly the gods sent him to us—the make-up artist, the best in Japan, we were told, and many others. Reporters had clamored to be present and were.

Our child actors were in their best party clothes, Little Setsu, Little Toru and Little Yukio, and their big dittos. Our entire cast, in fact, made me swell with pride. They were handsome, they suited their parts, and they were enthusiastic. Our co-producers were pleased, too, even the production manager. He stayed throughout the party, he made a speech in Japanese which was doubtless excellent, since there was loud applause. Our star, Sessue Hayakawa, also spoke in Japanese, the reporters took notes, cameras flashed again and again, and the party was on. There was plenty of food and drink and everybody soon knew everybody.

It was a lovely party. We were slow to part, and we said good-by with assurances that we would soon meet again and work together on *The Big Wave*. Tomorrow—tomorrow—and may all tomorrows shine as brightly as that one shone ahead, I told myself that night.

Again I did not wander forth alone into the night. Instead I opened the window and sent my secret message into space, with love. Wherever he is, he heard, or so I dreamed, for a new comfort descended upon my heart and brought to me my first intimation of eventual peace. It was his blessing.

Three

We arrived at the delightful town of Obama after a seven-hour journey by plane, train and car. It was midnight when we reached our hotel, and our beds, made Japanese fashion on the tatami mats on the floor, looked and were comfortable. It was a real Japanese hotel—food, plumbing and all, a big hotel, and in its way comfortable to the point of some luxury.

Again I was in a Japanese bed. A thick mattress laid upon the floor mats, a soft mattress, sheets and pillows and silk-covered quilt, all immaculately clean, provided the exact combination of hard and soft for the most restful sleep. There is, I think, a certain security in sleeping on the floor, perhaps because there is nothing to fall from. The restless sleeper may fling out arms and legs and even roll over and over, and he will be on the same level. It is the security the human creature always feels when he is on stable earth, a contact with the basic plain. Babies know it by instinct and sleep most soundly, therefore, when they sleep on their stomachs. Then, if they wake, or only dream, they feel hands and feet touch solidity instead of clutching at the air. However narrow the bed, if it is made upon the floor it seems spacious. And how sensible, too, the use of room! By day the bedroom is made into a pleasant sitting room, the bedding folded into closets, a wise use of space in a small and crowded country.

I slept well but woke early, eager to see the locations chosen for the filming of the picture. It had been late when we arrived, and I did not know what the views would be from the wide windows of the small veranda upon which my room opened. They faced south upon a curved bay, the bay surrounded by green mountains. The street lay between hotel and sea, and beneath my windows was a large pool of steaming hot water, natural heat, for Obama is a famous spa, with natural hot springs.

As soon as I stirred, the paper-covered shoji slid back and a pleasant little Japanese maid in a gay yukata, or cotton kimono, came in, knelt and bowed, and chattered in Japanese while she put away the bed. In a few minutes my bedroom was a sitting room, a low polished table in the center, cushions to sit upon, a backrest to lean against. The tokonoma alcove held a graceful vase of fresh flowers and a landscape scroll by a good artist.

"Breakfast," the maid told me in gestures, "very soon."

I nodded, and went down a flight of stairs to my private bathroom, and had a Japanese bath. The water in the little pool was the natural hot water and very refreshing, stimulating without being exhausting. And breakfast was an egg, some fruit, salt fish and rice. The mineral bath had made me hungry. After breakfast we set forth in a car. . . . Here I pause to say that the Japanese cars are as extraordinary as their drivers. They are adapted to an abrupt landscape and perilous roads. Japan has many good roads, far more than I remembered from early visits, but these cars go with equal spirit on rough narrow roads or cement and asphalt. Most roads are narrow and do not allow room for comfortable passage. Some, and not a few, allow for no passage at all. When two cars meet face to face on such a road, both stop. The drivers take stock of each other. Sooner or later one of them makes up his mind that he is the weaker and prudently he backs until he finds a corner where he can wait and let the other pass. A bus or a truck driver does not take stock. He simply waits for the other car to get out of the way, with an air of doing him a favor by not running him down over the cliff. There seems always to be at least one cliff on the side of every road in Japan and very often both sides overhang cliffs, without guard rails or protection. The reason, I suppose, is that when nearly every road runs at the top of a cliff above the sea, there is no use in dreaming about guard rails. People must learn to take care of themselves. The same principle holds true for driving through towns and villages and hordes of bicyclists. The result is that people do look after themselves and they teach their children to do so, and remarkably few accidents occur, at least in proportion to hazard!

. . . We drove for an hour through fantastically beautiful country and all my memories came alive, for I have lived on Kyushu for months at a time in an earlier incarnation. How well I remembered these sharply pointed mountains, accustomed to sudden mists of rain, and these indented shores and water-worn rocks, these villages sheltering in coves, the farm houses, their steep roofs thatched three feet deep, and the terraced fields, climbing step by step up the hillsides and even nearly to the tops of mountains! Nothing was changed. I put out of my mind the bomb-wrecked city of Nagasaki, which was very near, because the Japanese have put it out of mind, too, and have built a new city.

Later I did go to see it, and found it the new-and-old combination symbolic of all Japan these days—new, the monument erected in memory of those who died when the second atomic bomb was dropped; old, the house built on a hill where Puccini visited while he wrote *Madame Butterfly*. It is a tourist spot now, this house, and not well-kept and not even clean. Too many times has that story been told, and now it is quite out of date, for young western soldiers marry their Japanese sweethearts and if they do not, then Miki takes care of the babies.

And of old and new, nothing was more startlingly new than being invited almost casually one hot summer's day to greet the Emperor and Empress in the city of Fukuoka, a meeting impossible in the old days, when these two personages were as remote, not to say as improbable, as gods. That day in Fukuoka, however, we stood in line at the railroad station to welcome with bows the august ones. They descended from the train wearing western dress, and looking kind and somewhat weary. The Emperor might have been a not too cheerful business man and his wife a motherly and anxious helpmate, her dress long and her hat a problem. I wondered if they remembered with nostalgia the old days when they lived, remote and cool, upon Olympus.

I cannot deny that my heart beat faster as we approached the village of Kitsu, which was where our fisher boy, Toru, lived. Two hundred years ago Kitsu was wiped clean by a tidal wave. It was easy to see how it happened, for this small fishing village lies like a saddle between two mountains, the lesser one terraced straight up to the top and over. I must have been thinking of Kitsu when I wrote *The Big Wave,* so perfectly did this village fit the story. For after the tidal wave the people rebuilt again in the same place, these stubborn, brave Japanese people, and yet sooner or later their village would again be caught by a monstrous wave, and it is just as vulnerable today as it was two centuries ago, the houses the same shape and structure and set in just the same way, on the beach but with no windows to the sea.

I recognized it, every step, as we climbed down the narrow winding path to the village. Here were the houses, here the narrow streets not three feet wide, surely, down which no vehicle could pass, and scarcely two human beings. Down the worn stone steps we went to the sea, followed by twenty-nine children, exactly, for I counted them when we stopped at Toru's house. There it was, too, the house just as I saw it in my book, and even Grandfather was there, a lively cheerful old face, peering at us over the wall. He was past his fishing days and his sons and grandsons now carried on. His wife was dead, he told us, and his daughter-in-law and granddaughter tended the house and dried and salted the fish and carried the water up from the well on the beach.

We sauntered about the village and with deep content, because it was so exactly right, the fishing nets drying on the shore, the houses nestled between the terraced hills, a small old cemetery on one of them. There was even a flight of stone steps which we could use as the entrance to Old Gentleman's house on the mountain above. It was all impossibly true and right.

The hours had passed and it was time for luncheon. We ate at a restaurant famous for eel. There we climbed two flights of stairs to a big airy room where we ate broiled eel on rice and drank green tea and congratulated ourselves on our location for the film.

I feared to see our next location and I confessed my fear. It was to be the mansion of Old Gentleman, a scholar and a landlord, and could we find a family living in such a house who would be willing to lend it to us? There must be space and beauty and elegance, set in lovely gardens. I gave up hope privately and toyed with various makeshifts while we drove along a country road.

The impossible became the possible, however, as it does so often in Japan. The moment I saw the house from the road I knew it was Old Gentleman's house, no matter who lived in it. I entered the gate and found myself in a lovely garden. There were no flowers, for Japanese gardens are seldom flower gardens. A path made of wide irregularly shaped stones led to the main entrance and on both sides evergreens, low shrubbery, ferns and orchids not in bloom, made a landscape. At the door a lady stood. She wore a handsome dark kimono and she bowed low. We bowed in return, to the best of our American ability, and I asked if I might see the rest of the garden. There was a pool, not large, but so designed that it presented the aspects of a lake. There was a bridge leading into a narrow path and a pavilion set among the trees. I saw everything from the point of view of Old Gentleman. It was exactly the sort of garden he would have, and I half expected to see him waiting in the house.

He did not appear, however. There was only the handsome lady who welcomed us into the house, and she led us from one room to another, each spacious and decorated with taste. The farmhouse was three hundred years old, but this was the landowner's house and it was built only about forty years ago, to replace the older one. Old Gentleman, whoever he is, was a man of wealth and taste. These were his chosen pieces of furniture and the art objects in the tokonoma alcoves were his choices, too. Two of the rooms were furnished with carpets laid on top of the tatami and with chairs and tables, western style, but we ignored the modern aspects of Old Gentleman and stayed by his Japanese side.

Now the lady introduced us to her daughter, a young woman not half so pretty as the mother, and wearing western dress, which did not suit her. But she, too, was kind and I was touched and warmed to the heart when, after I had made my speech of appreciation, I heard them both protest that they considered it an honor to have their house used in my picture, and the lady said she would like some day to perform the tea ceremony for me. I accepted with thanks, and then she served tea in bowls so small that I knew the tea was precious before I tasted it. It was indeed the perfect tea, seldom set before westerners. I could not bear to drink it and have it gone, and yet it was so delicious, so far beyond any tea I usually taste, that I could not but sip it while I praised it. She was moved by my appreciation and brought in the small valuable teapot and poured thimblefuls of the elixir. It was of course the rare tea made from the first tender leaves of the tea plant in spring. An ounce of it costs an American dollar, which is much Japanese money. I am sure she did not serve it often even to Japanese guests. That she did so for us meant that she gave a gift. I received it as such.

And as we talked, I in English, she in Japanese, through an interpreter, she asked if she could record the conversation through an interpreter for her son, who is studying English. I said of course, and was amused to see concealed until now behind a couch a very modern tape recorder!

We said good-by at last, with many bows, promising to return soon, promising to be careful and break nothing in the house and spoil nothing in the garden. She was very gracious and begged me to leave the hotel and live with her, but I said I must stay with the company, thanking her all the same.

Now there remained the farmhouse and the empty beach to be seen. The beach could wait, for the day was darkening, but the farmhouse we must see. We drove past a village and between fields and road I recognized it. The farmhouse stood among terraces, itself built on a wide terrace, the road in front of it twenty feet above the rice paddy below. A wall of ancient brick ran across the front, but the wide wooden gate stood open and I walked into the world of my story book. Yes, this was the house, simple but spacious, wooden walls, rooms divided by shoji, a thatched roof so old that grass and flowers grew on it. Chickens, a goat, a little vegetable garden, some ornamental shrubbery, a few decorative rocks, a fine old-fashioned kitchen, a narrow veranda, a small pool for washing rice and vegetables, the farmer himself, a cheerful widower with a married daughter looking after him—it was exactly right. And, best of all, the farm family was friendly and eager to be helpful. When were we coming? Tomorrow? Good—good—the house was ours. Yes, they had electricity—and a pump in the kitchen, modern farm, the farmer said proudly. And he would be glad to have Americans see how he managed everything. Tea, please, before we left! It was night before he would let us go, and work began at seven o'clock the next day. Every hour of light is precious when a film is made on location.

The chickens, I noticed as I left, were of the most articulate variety. Only the darkness silenced them. Their dissonant cackling, their exclamations of excitement and outrage when we moved in the next day, were to be the background music of every scene we filmed at the farmhouse.

We were delayed, alas, and by rain—rain—rain. By the

time we reached our hotel that night, the rain was falling. I had feared rain, always the hazard of filming on location, especially in the climate of southern Japan, where sea and mountain are close neighbors. If the wind blows from the sea the sky will clear; if from the land, it will rain. This I remembered from days long past, and while I lay in my Japanese bed listening to the rain and waiting for sleep, I pondered on the strange divisions of my life.

How incredible, above all, that for the whole first half of my life, I did not know he existed! When I was here before, where was he? And now when I am here again, where now is he? Between these two eras were twenty-five good years of life together, a gem set into eternity before and after. And the old question beset me again, as it besets every human being who has known death come too near. I set my teeth against the inexorability of death.

Is there life beyond?

I remembered the courage of his atheism. How often we argued of the future in which one of us must live alone! For it would have been too good to be possible that we should die at the same moment and hand in hand cross the invincible barrier. I had known for years that it would be I who would be left, I with the heritage of long-living ancestors on both sides of my family. The question was should I remind myself of the possibility of life beyond or thrust it aside and live as though eternity were now—which it is, in one sense, there being no beginning or end in the endlessness of all things. So what then is the present solitude in which I am living? Is it an end to what once was, or is it a beginning to something I do not yet comprehend?

Did he know I was here in Japan? Was he still hovering about the house at home, the essence of himself, and were I there would I perceive his presence? Lying there on my

Japanese bed, the sound of the rising sea mingling with the rain on the tiled roof, I fought off the mighty yearning to go in search of him, wherever he was. For surely he was looking for me, too. We were ill at ease, always, when apart. But what are the pathways?

I remembered an evening at Sardi's, in New York. I was with a friend from Hollywood, and for the first time I met his wife. While her husband talked shop with other guests, this woman talked to me rather shyly, a pleasant Midwestern woman, not at all of Hollywood. She was timid at first and then upon some impulse she lowered her voice to tell me that she wanted some "real talk" with me. She had had, it seemed, a strange personal development in recent months. Her father, to whom she was very close, had lived with her for many years after her mother died, but had himself recently died. She worried about him, wondering if he were still himself somewhere, and if so, if he were happy, and in such worry she became depressed and was joyless.

One evening, she said, when her husband was delayed at work, she was sitting alone at her crocheting, a pastime to which she was addicted, and as usual, grieving over her father. Suddenly she heard him call her name, and looking up she saw him quite clearly across the room.

"You must stop this worrying about me," he had said in his usual practical voice. "I am all right—happy, in fact."

"Were you afraid?" I asked her.

"Afraid of my father? No!"

"But was he the same?"

"Exactly the same," she said, and then added, half puzzled, "Except I knew that, though *he* was there, his body wasn't."

"And have you seen him again?"

"Yes," she said, "several times, though I don't worry any more. Sometimes when Jack and I are just siting at home quietly of an evening, he reading and I crocheting, I'll feel somebody else is there and I'll see my father smiling at us."

"Does Jack see him?" I asked.

"I asked him once, 'Jack, do you see Dad over there?' He

said no, he didn't see him, but he believed I did, because in the old country where he came from there were people like me who could see beyond."

Yes, and remembering, I thought of what my fourteen-year-old daughter told me the day after the funeral. She had wanted his room after it was empty because it was next to mine and she slept there quite peacefully the first night, I remember, for I had asked her if she really wanted to sleep there so soon.

"I don't want the room to be empty," she said.

The next morning she said entirely naturally at breakfast, "Daddy came in last night. He looked wonderful—all well again and so cheerful. He just came back to see that everything was all right."

I restrained incredibility. "Did he speak to you?"

"No, just smiled."

"And what was he wearing?" I asked.

"I think it was his red velvet smoking jacket," she said.

But the red smoking jacket, though his favorite, had been laid away five years ago when he forgot about smoking.

Do I believe? If I do it is only because I believe that some day we shall know as we are known, and communications will be clear, the laws of science revealing to us the laws that govern the creating universe. Religion calls the creative force by a name, God for whom we wait. *En attendant Godot!*

There in the darkness of the night by the Japanese sea, I besought him to let me know by some true sign that he lived somewhere, only to tell me that he was. He made no sign. Yet silence is not finality. It may be only definition. He is there, I am here. We do not have the same wave length yet. Is that faith? I dare not call it so. I am trained in science. There are two schools in the approach. One is to believe the impossible an absolute unless and until it is proved the possible. The other is to believe the possible an absolute unless and until it is proved the impossible. I belong to the latter school. Therefore all things are possible until they are proved impossible—and even the impossible may only be so, as of now.

In this way my life continued to be lived on two separate levels, one by day, the other by night; one upon Earth, the other in search of a habitation not made with hands.

The rains fell, it seemed endlessly. It poured for three days without letting up. The mountains were hidden in rain and the sea roared against the rocks. We looked at one another in alarm. What if this went on and on?

"I thought you said June was the rainy season and this is September," the American said to me reproachfully.

I myself was somewhat startled by the downpour, and referred the matter to the Japanese *maître d'hôtel,* who said that June was always the rainy season.

"Then what is this?" I asked.

"It is just rain," the Japanese replied.

No one could deny the fact and so we passed on to more disputable matters. We decided to work on the script, planning each day's schedule, in case the rain stopped some day. Scene by scene and shot by shot we planned and we planned. It was necessary and constructive work, and I also learned what I did not know before, that for a motion picture one does not tell the story in time sequence. One shoots all the scenes at each location, regardless of where these belong in the narrative. Thus for the first four days we would stay at the farmhouse, shooting everything that had to do with the farmhouse and its family of four, Father, Mother, Yukio and Setsu. This seemed a confusing business to me, but I could see its logic.

We sat around the long low Japanese table together with our cameraman and our Japanese sound man and assistant to the director. We sat on the floor, of course, and the cameraman was so unwise as to choose one end of the low table. I say unwise because he has long legs, very long, and he could not stretch his legs out when he was tired of sitting on them, because I had already grown tired and my legs were already stretched out, crosswise, under the table.

Here I pause for a moment to discuss the matter of sitting on one's folded legs. Before I came to Japan this year, after so long a time away, I practiced faithfully every day folding my legs and sitting on my feet. It is not easy and at first I could only do it for three minutes and at best only got to twenty minutes, which does not last through a Japanese dinner, at least not the kind my friends give me. I was ashamed, but it was the best I could do. What was my pleasure, therefore, to discover that in the years I had been away, the Japanese have all but given up prolonged sitting on their legs! Instead they sit on chairs whenever possible, and the children, many of them, do not sit on their legs at all and even my friend said frankly that she could not sit for long in the Japanese fashion and anyway she thought it bad for the circulation. She attributed the surprising increase in height of this generation of young adults to the fact that they have not had to sit for hours on their folded legs. It may be the reason. Certainly I noticed the new height of the Japanese. The people are better looking and they have straighter legs.

Now let me speak of the cameraman. First I must say that he was charming, kind, temperamental and, in his field, an artist. He spoke little English but he understood much more than we thought he did. He was obviously devoted to his work, and wanted us to know that he had a special devotion to *The Big Wave,* which I believed he had, else why should he have worked with us? He was famous and could easily have earned as much on an easier job. But I was enchanted with him for other reasons. He was the most spectacular-looking human being that I had ever seen, very tall and very narrow in the feet, legs, body, arms, and hands, neck and especially face. He had a long, low-slung jaw and—but I cannot explain his anatomy. I do not know how he came to look like that. All I know is that I liked him, and I enjoyed his spectacular looks. There was so much in that long face of his that I looked at him again and again across the table. It was a sad face, I thought, and then again I thought it was not, so I kept looking at it. And our Japanese assistant was such a contrast, a very modern young woman in shirt and slacks and with a beehive arrangement of hair. She spoke foreign languages and she had studied ballet in Europe and she was newly married to our leading young actor, the grown-up Toru. His motion picture commitments prevented his being with us until the twenty-first, and so this was their first separation. She was teased a good deal by other members of the cast, and they forced her to write hourly postcards to her bridegroom, addressing them for her, and so on. She lent herself good humoredly to their fun, a calm young woman, intelligent and efficient and, incidentally, but importantly, very much in love.

Alas, upon the very day when it stopped raining and we had begun filming our first scenes at the farmhouse, our cameraman fell into a rice paddy. This was not as mild an event as it sounds, for it came at the end of a twelve-hour day. I had left location a little early in order to attend to some Tokyo business by telephone and was summoned to the hospital. There I beheld the elongated cameraman stretched on a bench in the hall, waiting to be X-rayed. We feared the worst, for he fell not only into the rice paddy outside the farmhouse, but the rice paddy was at the foot of a stone wall upon which the road ran, and he fell not as I had imagined, into soft mud and high rice, but upon rocks at the bottom of the paddy. His frame could best be defined at any time as a collection of very long thin bones connected loosely by withered brown skin, and lying on the bench he looked eight feet long.

We exclaimed our alarm but he refused to share it, and was carried into the X-ray room against his will. In half an hour the doctor reported no broken bones, only a bruise. The cameraman himself came out looking as gay as possible with his sort of a face, expecting our admiration, which we gave. He looked very smart in a clean black-and-white yukata, he had also permitted the doctor to put his right arm into a sling but only until he got out of the hospital, for he insisted upon returning to the job. We rode back to the hotel with him and gave him numerous orders, through our interpreter, that he was to have an attendant who would carry his chair everywhere for him to sit upon, together with a fan, an umbrella, cool drink and fruit.

The cameraman listened to this without change of expression and added, "And beddo."

We laughed and the indomitable old figure sat very straight on the front seat. We bade him good night at his hotel and so ended that day.

Here I must consult my notes, scratched on the pages of my script, and written everywhere and anywhere in the farmhouse, wherever the scene was being played.

The first note says, "Feather—"

Feather?

Ah yes, that is the scene where Toru lay in the long stupor after the tidal wave had struck, and mischievous little Setsu stole into the room and tickled him with a feather to wake him up. It was a pretty scene, interrupted by Mother who came in with eggs in a small basket, followed by our last addition to the cast, a small, very intelligent dog. A duck was the really last addition but he had not yet appeared on the set.

While this scene was taken, I saw Father in another corner rehearsing his big scene with Yukio. Father is a good farmer, his face an honest brown. Our make-up man, the best in Japan—or did I say that before?—was dabbing at Father's face and delicately wiping away the sweat of concentration. Mother's personal attendant was doing the same to her in another corner. The attendant provided us with laughter. She was so very efficient, rushing in at last moments before the camera began to call them, in order to set straight a hair on Mother's head and to add a touch of make-up to the corner of her eye or the edge of her lip.

"When work is over," my notes tell me, "it is a sight to see Mother in her elegant gray silk kimono wending her dignified way along the dirt road at the top of the wall above the paddy field. She is an actress of some distinction in Japan, Father acted in *Teahouse of the August Moon,* and Toru and Yukio are both child stars. I am proud of our *Big Wave* family."

That was the day, I remember, when the postman brought me a letter from a Japanese friend in Tokyo, a fellow writer, who had taken the trouble to go to the public library and collect some data on tidal waves from old family records. He wrote me that before a tidal wave rolls in there is a dreadful hollow booming from the sea. The Japanese call it the "ocean gun." And one sign of an approaching wave is that the wells go dry, or rise, and the water is muddy. And the fish, especially the catfish, swim toward land.

While I read the fascinating pages I heard the assistant director, a man, call the new scene.

"Yoi!"

"Hoomba!"

"Starto!"

"Backo!"

The actors took their places and the cameraman alerted. Then came the director's final command.

"Action!"

"Schis-kani," was said again and again during the scenes and I did not know what it meant until an electrician echoed it by roaring it in semi-English.

"Silento!"

The result was profound silence. And I was amazed by the simplicity of the mechanism. The microphone was something tied up in a cotton bag and suspended at the end of a bamboo pole and the end of the pole was always sticking into someone, as my own ribs could testify, but it worked well enough. When I listened to the sound track played back, I was surprised to hear how clear it was. Effects were achieved with strangely simple means. The camera, for example, was wrapped up as tenderly as a baby in a snowstorm in Central Park. I could not think why, for the weather was steaming hot, and surely the thing was not cold. Upon inquiry I learned that the blankets and quilts were to silence the noise of the camera itself so that the microphone would not pick it up.

Can it be that I have forgotten to tell how the city of Obama celebrated our arrival? Ah, but it took a little time. We arrived without pomp or circumstance in small Japanese cars, we unloaded ourselves and settled unobtrusively into the hotel. Moreover, we were all Japanese except the American director, his wife and child, and myself, and we were quiet folk, for Americans at least. In a day or two, however, word went about that we were there, that I was there, that a picture was to be made. The city fathers asked permission to call upon us, and we let them with pleasure. They came bearing huge bouquets of mixed flowers and with gifts of enormous flat sponge cakes, a specialty of Nagasaki, the nearest city. We invited them to drink tea with us, they accepted with pleasure, and begged us, through interpreters, to ask them for anything we needed.

"If you do not ask," they told us, "we will not know. Therefore ask!"

We promised, and tea drunk, they bowed and we bowed, and thus we parted.

The next day a large banner was hung on the wall of the main street, which in English and Japanese welcomed us to the city of Obama. The hotel, not to be outdone, made a similar banner, photographers took our pictures holding bouquets, and banners continued to wave during our entire stay. As time passed, a few letters faded in the sudden rains to which we were liable and in general the banners took on a spotted appearance, but the welcome, I am happy to say, remained as warm as ever.

And speaking of letters, I am reminded that Japanese school children are condemned to learn three languages, all Japanese. One is the ancient Chinese still used in formal writing, one Japanese phonetics, and the third the new language necessary in modern times, which is phonetic for English words incorporated into the Japanese tongue.

In spite of this linguistic burden, the children looked healthy and happy all day long except for the boy I saw on the way to our village, Kitsu. We turned an unexpected corner one day and came upon a robust and irate mother spanking the boy for some wrongdoing. She finished the job, in spite of our appearance, the boy howling as loudly as possible, then she dusted her hands, smiled at us cheerfully while the boy retired to a corner of the wall to finish off his sobs, and went back to her housework.

Should one spank children? I lingered behind the others on the narrow hillside path while I pondered the question. It was an old one in our American family, never settled. He said he believed in spanking children at certain ages because they were not open to reason and functioned entirely on instinct and emotion. I said I hated all physical punishment and believed it did no good. The difference between us was that when a child provoked me to anger, which in fairness to myself I must say was not often and only after outrageous provocation, I could and did find myself administering a swift and well-placed spanking. He, in spite of his belief in the principle, never had the heart to spank any child for any cause—except on one momentous occasion when I refused to have anything to do with it.

"The boys should be spanked," he told me one day, his face very grave.

I do not remember what they had done, but they had got into some devilishness together. They stood before us one fine summer's day, the three of them so near of an age, all handsome and healthy and unrepentant.

"I can't do it," I said.

"Then I will have to," he said firmly.

To our mutual astonishment, mine and the boys', he actually spanked each of them in turn. Grown men that they are now, they still roar with laughter when they talk of it together. They too do not remember what naughtiness they committed, but him they remember with love and amusement.

"We knew we ought to cry," the second son says, he with the gay sense of humor. "Just for his sake we should have cried, so that he'd have the satisfaction of knowing he was doing a good job, but it was so damned funny—we had to laugh."

I remember some sort of muffled noise and a pretense of rubbing their eyes with their knuckles and I was not fooled for one second. I knew they were laughing, bless them, and trying not to, because they did not want to hurt his feelings.

I suspected the Japanese boy of somewhat the same pretense. She was not hitting him very hard, and he was making a noise out of all proportion. Let my mother enjoy herself, he was thinking— Let her believe she is doing me good. . . . Let us, in short, be kind to our parents!

That evening, at my solitary dinner—it was a great scarlet crab—I found myself laughing aloud as I remembered. It was the first time I had laughed spontaneously alone since we used to laugh together and it was another milestone toward my new life.

The farmhouse was our first location and we worked there for days, each day like the one before. This was the pattern: I woke at half past five and went downstairs for my bath. The little maid, always watchful, needed no summons. While I was out of my room she came in and folded away the bed, set out the table and the cushion seat, and brought in my breakfast. This was, I must confess, the least successful meal of the day, made tolerable only by a special fruit that looked like an apple, but was a pear, not of the soft American variety but the crisp Chinese one. Two boiled eggs, thick toast and strange coffee completed the menu. I explained that I ate only one egg at breakfast and only one slice of toast, but explanations meant nothing. The company manager had ordered what I was to have and what he had commanded appeared. I suppose the little maid finished off the surplus, and I let it go at that.

In any case I had to be at the front door by seven o'clock. There we all gathered to exchange our slippers for our shoes, little maids waiting to help. Then we filled several cars, bowed to the assembled company of maids who waited to bow us away, and so we were off. The streets were clean, as everything is in Japan, the dust laid with fresh water and the cobblestones gleaming. The mountains pressing closely upon the sea were brightly green and the sea sparkled blue under the morning sun, if the day were fair. We drove through the city at reckless speed, passing hundreds of gaily dressed school children and out into the country on graveled roads between fields of ripening rice. There are times when I think Japan is the most beautiful country in the world. Yet it is the enchantment of Asia that every country is beautiful in its own way. We say *Asia*, and think in terms of a vast and swarming continent, the people indistinguishable one from another, but nothing can be more mistaken. The countries and peoples of Asia are as different one from the other as they can possibly be—more different than Americans are from Europeans. "That's for sure," as my Pennsylvania Dutch neighbors say. True, India and China are the two great mother civilizations, and their influence spreads into the neighboring lands and cultures, yet each land and each culture, acknowledging the influence, has nevertheless developed with individual and peculiar grace.

Arriving at the farmhouse, an appreciative audience awaiting us, we entered the gate every morning and found everything ready for us. The family had got up, put away their beds, made breakfast and departed for the day. From time to time some of them would come and see what we were doing, but courtesy forbade comment, whatever they thought. The surrounding villagers, however, frankly came to stare and they came in relays.

The first crowd, the early one, was always school children. Obviously they had risen early and were stopping on their way to school. They were mannerly and silent, their eyes unblinking. Precisely at a quarter past eight they left us in a body to begin school at half past. The next contingent were mothers, who by this time had put their houses in order and planned lunch. They arrived with babies strapped to their backs, and were not quite so mannerly. They could not refrain from whispered exclamations and laughter smothered behind their hands. They left, also promptly, at half past eleven in order to see that their working husbands were fed. About three o'clock grandparents and village elders arrived, after food and naps, to spend the rest of the afternoon with us. They were joined at five by the working fathers, whose day was done. These stayed with us faithfully until we left about seven.

On our part, we began filming as soon as the cameras were set up, moving from room to room as the story required. The make-up man and his assistant kept a zealous watch on the actors, lest the heat cause cream and rouge to run in rivulets down their faces and spot their costumes—a true artist and a charming man, our make-up man, with his secret formulas and brushes made by his own hands. I found one of those fine brushes on the beach after the work was over, and he had gone back to Tokyo, and I kept it for memory's sake. It is made of bamboo, splinter fine, and set with a narrow line of the best bristles.

Sound effects, throughout the day, were our bane. The ox lowed at the wrong time, the goat baa-ed too often, though merely to be friendly. As for the chickens, we gave up on them. Nothing could restrain them and consequently they will cackle happily throughout the farmhouse scenes wherever the film is shown.

The day's work went on until luncheon arrived from the hotel and we broke for an hour. The heat was frightening in August and we sat under the big persimmon tree in the front yard, a small space between the massive gate and the house, but there we all sat, some on the rise of the house, some on stones and stumps and sides of the cart. Each lunch was served separately and self-contained in a handsome lacquered box, the top layer containing fish and bits of browned meat, vegetable and pickle, and the bottom layer steamed white rice. Great pots of tea, with handles wrapped against the heat in thin strips of bamboo, completed our more than adequate meal. We ate with Japanese chopsticks, bamboo, sealed in waxed paper and thrown away after each use, surely the most sanitary eating utensils in the world.

In twenty minutes the meal was over and for the rest of the noon hour the farmhouse was quiet. Crew and actors were stretched out on the tatami, like sardines, asleep. I found a quiet ledge behind a little table, close by the back room, and lay looking out at the mountains lifted against the sky. White clouds floated against the blue and cast their floating shadows. It seemed a dream that I was here, that I was seeing my little book come to life in the country where it was conceived, my people now living Japanese people playing out my story.

That August heat! How restless the wild creatures were! Across the human voices the loud and ardent screech of a cicada shocked our sound man again and again. For me, it was a cry that summoned nostalgic memory of the hot summers of my childhood on the banks of the Yangtze River. Whenever the cicadas gave their screeching, seesawing cries, one knew that the summer was at its height. From then on we could only hope some day for a cool wind, even for a typhoon. The sound man, however, was furious with the cicada in the farmhouse yard. He shouted and half a dozen of the crew leaped at the big persimmon tree and knocked its branches with bamboo poles. For five minutes the lusty insect was quiet and then we heard its screech begin to saw the air. This time the men climbed the persimmon tree and shook it until leaves began to fall and the green fruit trembled. For at least half an hour the cicada was prudent and then it began all over again its endless song. But we were beset with other creatures. A proud cock announced the birth of every egg his harem laid. Chicks quarreled and squawked.

Among the ever-watching crowd, a baby cried and had to be removed.

One day we had a bit of luck. As our little Setsu came flying out of the farmhouse gate, her kimono sleeves her wings, the oldest woman in the world chanced to come by, bent under a load of sticks of firewood. She had a beautiful old face, wrinkled and brown, but her eyes were as young as life itself. We invited her to be in our picture, she accepted graciously and posed, straightening herself for the occasion and clinging to her tall staff while her gay old face assumed nobility. Our assistant make-up man in mistaken zeal rushed to arrange the folds of her kimono, which had fallen open to show a glimpse of ancient breasts, but we shouted at him to put it as it was before, and so we have her picture. She is walking along the road, bent under her load while the child Setsu runs past. We wanted to pay her, but were assured that it would hurt her feelings. The most that could be done with dignity was to give her some packages of cigarettes, which we did, and she went her way.

Rain and sun alternated through the days. Our actors worked well and they became a working group. We began to express the characters and we lived in the story. I remember one day that ended with the bringing home of Toru, after the tidal wave, when the young lad waked from his stupor, and inquired where his father was and where his mother. A sudden comprehending emotion swept the actors together. They knew, they understood all too well. Tears fell from the actress mother's eyes, and I felt a catch in my own throat for suddenly they had portrayed a moment of utter reality.

The last scene of that burning day was outside in the barnyard. It was nearly twilight, the crowd was now several hundred people of all ages. They ringed us around, always quiet and respectful, while the actors prepared the set, complete with cart, ox, produce and farm family. This time our family included Setsu's pet duck and her dog. The duck, which in the script is a little duck, in reality turned out to be a huge duck, the great-grandfather of all living ducks, and when our Setsu struggled to hold him under her arms I was reminded of *Alice in Wonderland* and the flamingo in the croquet game with the Duchess. The dog, a gay fox terrier type—although the tail was wrong, so I did not know quite what it was—would not gambol about harmlessly as it was supposed to do, but insisted upon chasing chickens madly, thereby upsetting a mother hen with a large family of chicks, not to mention an unknown number of white pullets, who apparently had never seen a dog before. The duck was carried off stage by Setsu, and the dog controlled and chastened and the scene proceeded.

At this moment I heard human cackles behind me as Father unloaded the cart. The cackles were hoots of laughter from two dirt farmers in the crowd who were overcome with amusement at Father's unrealistic handling of the pole and two baskets. They obviously did not believe in him as a farmer. As for Mother, when she appeared it was the women's turn to laugh. Not one of them was pretty, and Mother was pretty. So how could she be a farmer's wife? It was a question. Perhaps Mother was too pretty. But can a woman be too pretty in a movie?

The scene was over at last and we were getting ready for the next one, rushing against the darkness falling so fast in this hot climate, when suddenly I heard loud barks, as though from an immense and aged dog. I could not imagine what it was. There was no dog indigenous to the farm. I advanced to the stable to investigate and I smelled pig. It could not be pig, because it barked like dog. But it was pig, an enormous tough-looking old pig, male gender, barking like a cross old dog. I inquired through an interpreter why the pig barked like a dog when he was not a dog. The answer was simple. "We do not know why pig barks like dog." That was all. The pig continued to bark, the darkness fell, the assistant cameraman announced that we could not finish the next scene because the light on the mountain had faded. We gathered ourselves together and left. The pig stopped barking, the crowd ebbed away into the night, and we ebbed, too. Another day had passed. Tomorrow was a Sunday and we were to rest, although we had been warned that we were not to expect more Sundays off. From now on it was seven days a week, twelve hours a day. Sufficient unto the day—I thought only of bath and bed. Japanese bath and Japanese bed.

Such a wind arose in the night that I dreamed we were having a typhoon. The dream was a remnant of childhood, I suppose, or of former life upon the island, or perhaps only of *The Big Wave* itself, created by my own mind. Perhaps it was no more than a conversation the night before with the innkeeper's wife. This inn, she told me, had often been struck by typhoons, the last only last year, when the sea rushed into this very room, where I lived. At any rate, I woke, listening to the wind, and I remembered an August afternoon, long ago. I had stood upon a mountainside facing the sea, south of Japan. A typhoon was brewing somewhere over the horizon. We had been given warning and in all common sense I should have been safe inside a house with the windows battened down and the doors barred. No one knows what a typhoon will do. It is uncontrolled and therefore unpredictable. It is a release of senseless force and its only accomplishment is destruction.

I had seen many typhoons, however, in my Asian childhood and I had the wish, that day, to see one more. A typhoon is very much like a hurricane but the hurricanes I had seen in New England and Pennsylvania were not typhoons. The tropics or near tropics provide a volcanic power for wind and rain. We lived in a sub-tropical climate two hundred miles from the Pacific Ocean, and yet to this day I can remember my father's stern command and my mother's anxious face.

"There's a typhoon coming! Get the shutters barred and the doors locked!"

While the sky darkened and the first low growl of the winds rose into a sullen roar, we sat waiting and listening. Trees would break and walls would crumble and the house itself would quiver when the attack came, but we could do nothing except wait and listen. When it was over and silence fell at last, we opened the doors and windows. What we saw was always the same—destruction everywhere.

"Stupid," my mother would say. "So stupid!"

It was the memory of her invariable comment that had given me the idea of the typhoon for a story, and had sent me to the mountainside that morning long ago on a previous visit to Japan. The radio had announced a typhoon.

It had come just after one o'clock, preceded by a strange distant sound over the lifting horizon. I had taken shelter under the rock of what was a sort of cave, having made sure that this rock was part of the spine of the mountain and not some treacherous boulder to crash down upon me in the storm. I had made sure, too, that I was high enough on the mountain so that the sea could not reach me. And I had to take heed that there were no trees near by to fall upon me. All in all, I was as safe as a person could be who had decided upon risk.

There I sat, then waiting but this time alone and without family or house to shelter me. It was a profound experience, terrifying and rewarding, and it provided the scene I wanted for the beginning of the story. Let me describe it as best I can. The typhoon came out of the sea first as a deep hollow roar. Then it appeared as a monstrous black cloud. The cloud seemed a thing alive, shaping itself this way and that, torn by contending winds. However it might stretch to right or left, it continued to spread upward and reach toward east and west. The day darkened to twilight and the dreaded roar of sound came rushing toward me from out of the depths. I crouched behind my rock and waited.

At first, I remember, there was no rain, only the wild winds and the tossing sea. An hour earlier the sea had been calm and blue. Now it was black and streaked with crests of white foam. When the rain came it was all of a sudden, as though the clouds had opened and spilled. A curtain of rain fell between mountain and sea, a solid sheet of water three feet away from me. The grass and brush on the mountainside flattened under the wind and the rain. I was surrounded by the madness, the unreason, of uncontrolled, undisciplined energy. None of this made any sense. It was worse than useless—it was nature destroying its own creation—its own self. To create by the long process of growth and then to destroy by a fit of wild emotion—was this not madness, was this not unreason? I had the beginning of my story.

The storm spent itself at last. The winds dispersed, the rain slackened to a drizzle and a mist, the cloud fell apart and the sun shone through. I came out from my shelter and surveyed the ruin left behind. Trees had fallen on the lower levels, gullies were dug into the earth between the rocks, the very grass and underbrush lay flat and exhausted. I could only guess what havoc had been wreaked upon the villages along the coast, the fishing boats broken and tossed out to sea, houses smashed, breakwaters wrenched apart, sea walls crumbled. It was, as my mother had said, all very stupid. It was useless.

I have seen this same waste take place in human life, in human beings, in terms of human emotions.

I lay there in my Japanese bed, years later, and mused on the similarity of typhoon energy and energy of human emotion. Uncontrolled, it destroys. But must emotion be destructive? And if not, when is it valuable and why? How can we use emotion as helpful energy, necessary energy for living? What are the uses of emotion and what are the disciplines necessary for its helpful use? These were the questions I longed to answer, first for myself and then for others. I put myself first for I am the lens through which I view others.

And as always, when I cannot answer my own questions, I send my mind, my heart, in search of him. He could not answer, not always, but he had a talent for directing the search by questions of his own, skillful and enlarging. His was not a profound mind. I cannot pretend that he could always follow me in the search to the conclusions that come one by one, through which one proceeds not as absolutes but as steps toward truth. Truth itself is, of course, no absolute. Perhaps, indeed, it pervades the process, existing in everything and everywhere as eternally as time itself, a wholeness of which at any stage we see only part. He did not possess the conceptual mind nor had he the scholar's disciplines, in which I have been trained. It was understood that there was much that we could not share. Our natures were essentially different. Our enjoyments even in music and literature were unlike. We both loved music, for example, but I am happiest when I am working on a Beethoven sonata or with Chopin. He enjoyed lighter music, which I also enjoy, but only as caviar. On the other hand I am deeply interested in jazz, not so much musically as psychologically, and he had no interest in jazz on any terms. He had no interest, either, in science, although he did have an academic interest in technology. Since he was a determined atheist, he could accept but not share my unending involvement with theoretician physicists, and the tremendous significance of their recent discoveries.

What he did have was a brilliant intuitive mind, and what was more rare, the ability to appreciate what he could not comprehend. He stimulated by skillful questions, he seemed never to lead although he did not follow, he uncovered without shaping. He provided an atmosphere in which I could think more clearly, create more spontaneously than I might otherwise have been able to do. He could listen to me think aloud around and above and under a subject that interested me, allowing me to range freely as though I were alone, his questions never guideposts but invitations to pathways I might not have noticed for myself.

I realize that now, alas, I have no one with whom to talk. Be still, my soul!

The schedule called for outdoor work, a picnic scene with little Setsu and a harvest scene, then field and plowing but it was raining again. We proceeded nevertheless to within walking distance of the site, a charming place on a terraced hillside, and in the background a gray old Japanese cemetery. It was upon one of these stone graves that Setsu was to wait with food for Father and Yukio, with what disastrous and naughty results I must not here tell. The contrast of the mossy old tombstones and our pretty little girl was the contrast of life against death and I had looked forward to the scene. We waited in the cars while the rain poured down. A kind farm family invited us to shelter in their comfortable house, and we went in, gratefully. The farm wife prepared tea for us, and we discussed what to do. Mountains and sea here combined to make weather a mystery even more uncertain than in most parts of the world. The sky looked as though it would continue to empty itself for forty days. We decided to go to the farmhouse and shoot a rain scene, appropriately, and a kitchen interior. The assistant director was to go to Kitsu, our fishing village, and get boats ready for the scene when the boats put out for the shark beach in the rain.

The morning was a disappointment, nevertheless. The rain continued into deluge. The farmyard became a lake of mud and the thatched eaves dripped dismally. Inside the farmhouse the crew worked without enthusiasm. The cameraman put off evil moments of beginning work, the director grew impatient and I grew bored. Again and again the first scene was set and again and again the camera made some monstrous mistake. It was twelve o'clock by the time we were ready to shoot the rain scene, and then the sun came out, weakly but enough to make it necessary to fake rain. So on a rainy day the men climbed on the farmhouse roof and rigged up the best rainmaking machine in the world, namely, a hollow bamboo pierced with holes, with a rubber hose attached to one end and the other end stopped. A beautiful flow of fake rain dripped over the eaves and down into the lake of mud made by the real rain. Finally we got a take, and lunch hour arrived. The day was so dismal it was not even a good lunch.

The kitchen scene and the rainy beach scene were among our best. The kitchen scene was the earthquake. Our farm mother, in a daze, hurried about, trying to save her dishes. She was so distraught that she forgot to put down a basket of eggs and they broke and increased the confusion. There is, in fact, nothing more confusing than a basket of broken eggs, especially when a woman forgets to put them down before she rushes around her kitchen trying to save her dishes during an earthquake, and sees in addition that the oil lamp is burning and may set the house on fire. It was quite a scene and in her reality of acting our mother cut her foot twice on broken glass and the trained nurse, whom we were required to have with us at all times, at last had a chance to save someone's life. She came forward with an air of importance and put some adhesive tape on Mother's foot. We were impressed by this efficiency and felt somewhat cheered.

Sheer stubbornness prevented me from giving up and wending my muddy way back to the hotel, and I was glad. With that inexplicable upturn which seems inevitable when the worst arrives, the afternoon work suddenly became exciting. The farmhouse actors were dismissed for the day and the fisherman's family summoned for the beach scenes. The rainy scene finished, the sun had withdrawn and again rain fell in deluge. It became apparent now that the American director had every intention of dismissing me, too, on the grounds of the storm, rain, lashing waves and so forth. When I declined to be dismissed he put forth vague suggestions that I might break a leg or something on the steep and narrow path down to Kitsu, and he had had enough of falls. I refused this ridiculous reasoning, for my two favorite houses are in the countryside of Pennsylvania and the mountains of Vermont, and I walk prodigiously everywhere and climb like a goat—female—and never have slipped or fallen, unless someone dropped me as a baby, which I do not remember. I invited this director to pay no attention to me except to check before going back to the hotel in the evening in order to see that I was in some car or other, and so I went to Kitsu.

I shall never cease to be grateful that I did, for the experience gave me—well, here it is:

I walked down the narrow winding cliff path without mishap, and descended to the beach, ostentatiously and unobtrusively pretending that I was not there. It was raining gloriously, a rough downpour, which I love. I was protected thoroughly by my raincoat and hat, and also by various umbrellas held over my head by kind villagers. My only complaint in Japan is that people are so kind that I always find an umbrella over my head, a fan in my hand, and a stool where I sit. While the director shaped up his scene and peered into the camera, I stood with my back to the high wall in front of Toru's house and gazed out over the gray sea and gray sky. Our actor, Toru's father, was a fisherman, and at the signal he began to blow the great conch shell for the boats.

"Cut!" the director yelled.

We cut. All the village was out under huge umbrellas to watch what was going on and some unwary boy had dashed across the scene to a better place on the other side. The village headman, who was our paid ally, had forbidden noise or movement, and at this he went into a fine paroxysm of fury. I speak and understand no Japanese, but I could see that he was calling his fellow villagers a lot of damned blockheads and did they want to show the world what idiots they were, not knowing that when you cross a camera you ruin the picture being made by Americans here in the village of Kitsu for the first time in history, a place unknown to the world until now as the home of children and fools? They all grinned sheepishly and fell back six inches or so. Suddenly another boy who had not been listening dashed between the frightfully bowed and hairy legs of the headman himself, not remembering to fold his umbrella first. The results were disastrous, the umbrella was ruined.

Here I pause for a moment to remember fondly that headman in the village of Kitsu. He had a round, shaven head, a rugged, beaming face, legs as crooked as a crab's, an iron will, and a heart fit for a king. He was a dictator, of course, and he ruled his people absolutely. Every night he told them what they could do the next day and what they must not do. Thus after the reprehensible behavior of the boys, the villagers were forbidden to stare at us or hang about. They were to continue their usual duties as though we were not there, except, as a special favor, for one hour between five and six in late afternoon and then they must stand no nearer than fifty feet away to watch us, and in total silence. His enthusiasm for the picture was touching for he was convinced that the story is about him. Like Toru, his entire family was swept away by a tidal wave when he was only a little boy.

Standing there, my back against the wet sea wall, I watched the cameraman get a lovely shot of fishermen carrying their nets and running down to the sea and putting off in their fishing boats through the waves and rain. Camera then raced to the big breakwater, which made an ideal platform from which to film the boats driving into the open sea. The villagers rushed after the camera and I was swallowed among the crowd. I was all but pushed off the breakwater into the sea, which would have made the director so eternally right that I daresay I would have had to take the next plane home in order to escape the wrath of God. But I was fortunately saved by a strong villager who breathed warmly into my face—he had halitosis, alas, and of the fiercest sort, a pity, for he was such a nice man. He told me, breathing hard, that he saw me on the Tokyo television and may he hold his umbrella over my head, and why isn't someone looking after such an important person as I am? I said that no one ever looked after me when pictures were being made, and thanks, I don't need the umbrella because I have a rain hat and so I escaped him to go and sit upon a stone pier and watch the matchless beauty of Japanese fishing boats putting out to open sea.

I skip all the dull routine of their being told to come back and do it over again because of the cameraman's locking the camera so that he could not pan and then his thinking something was wrong with the camera and the American saying bitterly that the only thing wrong was the cameraman, and all such small talk. Let me tell only of sitting there in the rain, that slanting rain which Hokusai loved so well to portray in his prints. Surrounded by the green and terraced hills and the higher mountains swathed in clouds, and gazing out over the endless sea, I watched for the boats to return and saw them as they rounded the end of the breakwater. How beautiful they were, how superb in shape and speed and grace! Three men sat in each boat, all rowing, not the choppy rowing of western boats, but smoothly as a fish swims, these rowers never lifted their oars from the water. I studied the rhythm of those oars. It was in contrapuntal thirds, no oar moving at exactly the same instant as the other, and yet all movement flowing. Suddenly I recognized the rhythm—it was that of the fins of a fish. The boats moved through the sea as a fish moves by its fins. I felt the deep satisfaction of right conclusion. That is exactly what it was and I was slow not to know it until this late date in my life, although I have been watching such boats since I was a child, spending my summers in Japan.

The boats put out to sea again in a long row. They turned to the left as the bay turns until they were hidden by a rocky point, upon which stood by accident the figure of a man, solitary and unknown, looking toward the horizon. What beauty! It is enough for this day. I thank God, and may I see beauty all my life as clear as this!

I went back in grateful silence, I remember, and had my bath and dinner. The bathroom was big and two small windows, opaquely glazed, opened to the pool outside. I could hear the swimmers shouting and laughing while I bathed. Floor and walls of white tile, and the tub was a square of tiled cement four feet square and as deep, one end raised to make a seat and so keep my head above water. It was always full of hot mineral water, soothing to the skin. But why do I talk of the tub? I knew better than to step into it without the proper preparation, which was to fill a small wooden tub with water, sit upon a small bamboo stool in the middle of the tiled floor with the little tub before me, soap myself thoroughly, and pour water over myself. Only then was I fit for the big tub. When I stepped out of it every ache and touch of fatigue was gone. I was mended, and I was renewed.

That evening I sat by my window, I remember, dressed in a cool yukata, and heard the swimmers in the pool outside plunge and shout and laugh. I had that day been steeped in beauty, and now it was unbearable because I could not tell him about it. Perhaps he knew—but if he could not communicate his awareness to me, how was I to be comforted? I had, I thought, been doing so well and suddenly I knew I had not.

"It does not get better," a widowed friend had warned me. "It gets worse."

What does *worse* mean? How could it be worse than this? I wanted suddenly to wipe away all remembrance of beauty, and yet I am one who cannot live without beauty—and I do not allow myself to weep. I thought I had been doing well. I felt he must be proud of me, if he were watching somewhere, afar off. Now I needed help again and badly. Where to find it? Beauty had undone me, had made me weak with longing. Strangers must again be my refuge. I took off the yukata, slipped into my own dress and went to wandering on the streets again, alone.

Not far from the back door of the hotel, down a narrow cobbled street, I discovered the motion picture theater. It was the only one in town, and a very good one, the stage spacious, the seats comfortable. As a courtesy, the owner had sent word that we were to enter without tickets so long as we were in Obama, and as the days passed I grew into the habit of slipping across the street in the cool of the night, and choosing a seat beside a red-lacquered pillar. Around me were the Japanese crowd, mostly men, since there were no bars in Obama and this was perhaps their only relief from crying children and over-burdened wives. True, there were three old geisha in the city but they were more or less honorary and had become respectable members of the community now that they had retired from active business. Certainly they could not be considered sources of relaxation for tired business men.

The pictures were revelatory. The mildest and most artistic films in Japan, I fear, are those sent abroad for foreign consumption. The real stuff is kept at home and especially for the remoter areas, of which we in Obama were certainly one. Emotions on the screen were violent, primitive, repetitive and for me highly amusing. Everything was over-colored, literally as well as symbolically. The reds were the color of blood, the greens poisonous, the blues sulphurous. Equally extreme was the action. One rape was never enough for a single film. I sat through evenings when the same girl was raped two and three times by one man or by various men. Gun shooting, obviously copied from our wild-western shows, was far more wild. Everybody shot everybody until only one man remained and then he shot himself. A good evening's entertainment seemed to be when all the women were raped and all the men killed. The audience then gave a sigh of happiness and rose in a state of dream to return to their wives and children. Yet these same men were always delicately courteous to a stranger and gently polite to one another. The Japanese nature is not so much complex as simply contradictory.

Reflecting upon the raw emotions I observed without sharing, it seemed to me that jealousy was the predominant passion, with rape and murder the inevitable result. I would laugh at this, except that I now recall an incident in my own household, known as the Affair of the Wooden Plate.

We went to Scandinavia one year, he and I, on a combined pleasure and business trip and stopped in Copenhagen to visit some friends. At dinner on our first night I admired some beautiful wooden plates and expressed a desire to purchase a dozen for our Pennsylvania home. This I did, the very next morning, and had them sent off direct. When we reached home the twelve wooden plates were already there, unpacked and waiting, and they were even more beautiful than I had remembered, and we used them at our first breakfast. The children had got up earlier that morning and had breakfasted with their nurse, since we had arrived late the night before. There were only the two of us then, he and I.

For years after that breakfast my children, my housekeeper, and other odd persons persisted in asking me why there were only eleven wooden plates and for years I was vague in my replies. Eleven plates? Were they sure there were only eleven plates? I must count them myself—et cetera.

The truth is that I knew there were only eleven wooden

plates. When he and I began breakfast that morning there were twelve but when we finished there were eleven. This is how it happened—and I begin by saying that it is wonderful and by the grace of God that a fault in one's beloved is no impediment to true love. Thus I acknowledge that this was his only fault—or nearly his only one, except that, as I have said he could not hammer a nail without banging his thumb black and blue, so that he sensibly followed my advice and gave up hammers entirely. This only fault then, was jealousy! At first it made me laugh, since I have never understood jealousy. If he, for example, had fallen in love with someone other than me, or had simply been temporarily attracted, I cannot imagine myself being jealous. If the beloved can find something better than he already possesses, how can one have the heart to deprive him of that joy? As for temporary attraction—well, one can always think about something else while it goes on and there are many enjoyable pursuits for which life provides all too little time. Music can fill twenty-four hours a day, so can sculpture and gardening, especially roses and camellias—so can reading and writing and improving the looks of one's house and walking through the woods and motoring and flying and swimming and sailing in ships and, above all, conversation with interesting persons.

Alas, it was the last occupation which caused the trouble. I cannot resist interesting persons and some of these are men, though whether they be men or women is not the point with me. A good mind is equally fascinating whether the containing skull box be male or female. Not so with him. He, the calmest and coolest and wisest of men, could be absurdly jealous if the brain that attracted me were in the skull of a man. I say absurd, for that is how it appeared to me at first. I had no intention of limiting conversation to women and said so. I made a joke of the whole thing, but he did not laugh. This astonished me and then annoyed me, but I concealed my annoyance as gracefully as I could.

During our journey in Europe he had been better than usual, and I had talked with many interesting people without thinking of consequences. On that particular first morning home we talked as we ate, laughed over certain past events, and enjoyed ourselves as usual. It was a lovely morning, the sun shone on our breakfast table, the bowl of roses spread their fragrance, and we had our own fresh eggs and homemade bacon. I had just admired the effect of the bacon and eggs on our Chinese blue plates under which were the wooden plates we had bought in Copenhagen, whereupon that dear and usually predictable man looked at me across the table and stopped laughing. I looked at him, surprised, and saw his heavenly blue eyes begin to turn green.

"What is wrong?" I exclaimed.

"These plates," he said. "They remind me of that day in Copenhagen."

"So why–" I began and was stopped.

His voice was steel cold. "The way you talked to–the way you smiled at–"

Now I stopped him, but not by words, I was far too furious for that. I am not an angry woman, nor a contentious one, nor argumentative. I am called soft-spoken, I believe, by newspaper reporters. They are right. I am soft-spoken and even gentle, in a tough sort of way. Also I was trained in the Confucian tradition that a superior person never speaks or acts in anger. That morning, however, and at that moment, I forgot all about Confucius and superior persons. True, I did not speak in anger because I was too angry to speak at all. I went blind and dumb with anger and purely by instinct I lifted the wooden plate with blue china plate, and my bacon and eggs upon it, and smashed it on the floor. The destruction was total, for our dining room has a brick floor. Then I walked out of the house and across the meadows and down into the woods. There I sat on a log by the brook. I sat there for three hours and thought over my whole life, examined my marriage, and weighed the advantages and disadvantages of being in love. By that time all anger had departed, I could laugh, and was fit to live with again. I walked back home refreshed and hungry, since I had not eaten my breakfast before anger. I found him sitting grimly at his desk, trying to work, and I could see clearly enough that he had been exhausted by not coming to find me. We flew into each other's arms, he stammering something about forgiveness, but I would have none of that. When we were calm again, he said so humbly that my heart half broke, for humility was never a part of his nature,

"Shall I write to—"

"Don't mention his name," I said in sympathy.

"But shan't I order another wooden plate?" he asked, still humble.

"No," I said. "Let there be eleven wooden plates forevermore. Because if you should, just once, forget, I'll count the plates out loud for you to hear—one, two, three, four, five, six, seven, eight, nine, ten—*eleven!*"

The end of this story is that we lived happily ever after and I never had to count the plates again, not even once. And I have continued all interesting conversations everywhere in the world and with anyone.

The day we changed location to the mansion that was Old Gentleman's house was one of the perfect days. Sometime after midnight I woke to a new air. The heavy heat of the land wind was changed suddenly by a west wind from the sea. This air was crisp and clean and meant sunshine in the morning. To such a morning we woke. The mountains were free of mists, the sun was shining, the world was new. We climbed into waiting cars, sharply on time, and drove along the cliffs to Old Gentleman's house. Far below us, as we made the big curve, fishing boats were drawing in the nets, a circle of white dots pulling closer and closer. I say the big curve, for the road seemed always to overhang the cliffs. Just at the point of the curve there was a shrine, and upon the shrine there stood a little stone god, a warning to careless drivers, someone to plead and protect. I passed him every morning and if it was not dark, then every evening, too.

Old Gentleman's house was near the town of Issahaya, a busy small city, very clean as all Japanese cities are, and with many prosperous-looking small town shops. There were more than a few pottery shops, for the famous Arita ware is made near here, but neither town nor shops engaged our attention at that moment. Just ahead was the house, its tiled roofs shining with dew under the morning sun. It was a stately house, surrounded by a wall, and the entrance gate was imposing, two great wooden doors fastened with iron hasps and hinges, and to the right a small wicket gate barely wide enough to admit one person.

The gates were open, for our crew had already arrived, and when we entered we found the western furniture put away and only the beautiful old Japanese things ready for our picture. The master of the house was at home today, a sturdy man in a dark kimono. With him was his wife and they greeted us kindly and warmly. With them were the two daughters, one in her twenties and another in her teens. They too were welcoming and warm.

Nevertheless I wondered if the family knew what it was in for. Our amazingly efficient crew had simply moved in, carpenters and electricians and make-up men and whatnot, and in a moment what had been a peaceful old-fashioned elegant home had become a sort of factory, in spite of the care the men took in doing no damage. Sheets of matting were laid over the fine tatami, and under the clasps that fixed the electric klieg lights to the ceilings the crew put a protection of soft paper. The ceilings of the house were beautiful, a copper-colored wood with a satin-soft finish. But everything was beautiful. Between the rooms and along the verandas fine bamboo curtains bound with satin provided decoration as well as screen. In each room the tokonoma alcove had its special scroll and flower arrangement. The table and utensils for the tea ceremony stood in a special room and panels in the wall opened to reveal a Buddhist shrine shining in gold leaf. The gardens outside were not large but they were well-landscaped and the big flat stones of the walks were arranged with skill and artistry. Our men were busily putting seaweed moss along the edges and in the cracks of the front walk, and they did such a good job that I thought the seaweed was real moss until I was told it was not.

When we were ready, we all sat and waited for our star to

arrive, our Old Gentleman, Sessue Hayakawa. He had dined with us the night before and, in western dress had looked like a handsome young man of fifty. We had discussed old age and he told us he practiced yoga and expected to live to be a hundred. Whether yoga has anything to do with it I do not know, but his family do live to be over a hundred—it is a tradition with them, it seems, and they feel cheated if they die before they complete a century. Sessue Hayakawa said his grandmother had died when she was only ninety-nine and her relatives felt she had let the family down. Having gone so far, they thought she should have braced up and finished the century as her forbears had.

Sessue Hayakawa was soon ready to perform, and looked stunningly handsome in the garb of an old-fashioned conservative Japanese gentleman. We examined his make-up, and pointed out to the make-up man a hair out of place in his beard and that the edge of his mustache had come slightly unglued. Sessue's secretary-maid, or maid-secretary, fanned him all the while, lighted his cigar or cigarette, gave him tea, and generally consoled him. She was young and efficient and took care of him as though he were a nice old baby, which perhaps he was. Whatever he was, he was also a professional actor and a star and it was a joy to see him at work. He gave himself to his part, and gained stature as the day went on. After lunch his aide fetched cushions for him and a pillow and he stripped to his undergarments, all white silk, and lay down and slept in yoga calm while the crew milled about him.

We were without our two boys that day, I remember—Yukio and Toru. They had gone to Nagasaki the day before, had drunk Japanese beer and eaten Chinese food, which is not a good combination. Hence they were ill in the night, and could not appear on the set in the morning, whereupon our star complained that he could not act without them and for a moment the day looked bleak. Then he relented and said that if he had a young girl from the cast to inspire him, he could act. So we lent him our little Transistor girl until the boys arrived, and she sat at the foot of the camera and looked appealing and pretty and he proceeded with relish and gusto.

I remember that entire day as pure joy. The air was light and cool, the sun brilliant. We were all in a state of euphoria, I think, sharing the pleasure of the beautiful surroundings and the smooth grace with which the work went on. Old Gentleman was growing before our eyes. It was like watching a great artist paint a portrait. Yes, I see, as though the scene were here and now before my eyes, the spacious Japanese room, the shoji open to the lovely garden. There before the window Old Gentleman in his white silken robes, scholar and aristocrat, poet and prophet, is sitting upon a cushion before a low table. He is brushing upon a wide sheet of paper the letters of a poem.

The children of God
Are very dear,
Very nice, but very narrow.

Before him kneel the two children. He reads the poem aloud and asks them what it means. They do not know, and he explains slowly and with a grave dignity.

The dialogue is in English and his English is not perfect, but he is able to convey the meaning and the atmosphere of his own soul. The children respond to the illusion of reality. I go smiling all day after that. The evening approaches and I am filled with content and expectation. The high point in the story now has arrived, the hour when Old Gentleman knows that the tidal wave is near. He orders the big bell to be rung and the torches outside the gate to be lit, the final warning to the people to come up the mountain to his house so that they may be saved, they and their children. He fears —he all but knows—that they will not heed, but it may be that a few will come.

It was dark when we assembled for this final scene and I live it again as I write, and let me continue to use the present tense. A great crowd has gathered from the villages and countryside. The day is over and people are free to come and watch what is happening on the hill. A platform has been built across the road at a suitable distance for the camera, and facing gate and house. On either side of the gate great torches are laid ready to be lit. The company manager, a burly fellow with a trumpeting voice, comes out and addresses the crowd, adjuring them to make no noise. It is the big scene, he tells them. There must not be a cough or a cry. The crowd shouts back promises and continues to wait. Endless time passes somehow while last touches are made. The make-up man is frantic, Old Gentleman has to wear a high ancient hat, his beard must be fast so the wind cannot blow away a hair. Even the servant must be made-up with care.

I am given a folding chair under the high platform and there I sit in quiet excitement to wait and watch. The last words are given, the assistant shouts his "get–ready, get–set," and the director says "Action!"

We begin. I watch with a mighty tightening of the heart. I can scarcely breathe. I remember when I wrote that scene and when it was finished I was exhausted. Now I am to see it in life. Will Old Gentleman be able to play it as I wrote it? Is it possible that he can do it with the power and majesty that were revealed to me?

Behind me and on the patio between the surrounding rice fields the crowd stands silent and absorbed. The crew is busy with lights and camera and suddenly the strong glare falls upon the old servant coming out to light the torches. The leaping flames flare in the darkness to reveal Old Gentleman, that proud old man, standing at the top of the stone steps to the gate. He is gazing out to sea. He is desperate, that old man, a prophet unheeded, yet yearning. He sees all too well what will happen to his people, his ignorant, stubborn and beloved people. Yes, yes—he is the character I created. I see him clear and whole, perfect in conception and detail, and am surprised to feel tears running down my face —I who never weep!

Such realization comes seldom to an artist—a few times perhaps in a lifetime of creation. To me it now comes perfectly for the first time, the happy coincidence of creation made manifest in the flesh and the mind of another human being. I am overcome with the need to share the moment with someone—someone! Hundreds of people are crowding around me, kind people but at this moment strangers. Among them there is no one. I turn and walk through the darkness to the waiting car and am driven away into the night.

In that moment I realized what before I had only known. He was dead. There was to be no further communication. Had communication been possible it would have come by some means out there in darkness when I was alone in the crowd. He would have heard me, he would have known my need. Whatever the barriers, he would have found the way to me somehow, had he been awake and aware, wherever he was. He had always found a way. That he did not could only mean that communication was now impossible or that he was neither awake nor aware.

The hotel room became intolerable again. I slipped unseen through empty corridors and walked the silent streets of the town. All decent folk were in bed, and even a drunken man was staggering his way home. The moon was full—somehow a month had passed—and by its light I left the town and went out into the country. Silence, silence everywhere and only silence, because death is silence. I do not know how long I walked or how far, or even where, except it was beside the sea, so calm that there were no waves, only the long swell of the deep tides. I remember how beautiful the landscape was, by night, the mountains rising above silver mists in the valleys. I saw everything and felt nothing. It was as though I were floating and far away, in a strange country in which I had no life. I might have been dead myself, so profound was the silence within. I would never weep again. I knew now there was no use in tears, nor any comfort to be sought or found. There was only this one—myself. Silly to cry for myself!

I turned inland from the sea then and was walking along a narrow path between rice fields. The air was windless until suddenly a wind rose from nowhere, it seemed, and I stopped to feel the freshness on my face. At that same moment I heard a child cry, a baby, I could tell by the high frantic agony. I looked about me. Yes, a farmhouse across the field was bright with lights. Was the child ill? I have heard so many babies cry that I know their language. No, this was not agony—surprise, perhaps, fear, even anger. It was the cry of a newborn child.

I sank down on the grassy bank, listening. The crying stopped, and I heard voices and laughter. The child was a boy, then! The child was another life. I lay back on the grass as though upon a bed and for a long time gazed up into the sky. The stars were not visible, for the bright moon was swinging its arc across the heavens and I watched it until I could believe I saw it move. A desperate weariness was creeping into my bones, the weariness of acceptance, the acceptance of the inescapable, the conviction of the unchangeable. From now on I must never again expect to share the great moments of my life. There would be such moments as long as I was alive, moments of beauty, moments of excitement and exhilaration; above all, moments of achievement. In such moments he and I had turned to each other as instinctively as we breathed. That was no more to be. . . . It is not true that one never walks alone. There is an eternity where one walks alone and we do not know its end.

The night was over and in the east beneath the horizon the sun was shining. It was time to go back to my room, time to prepare for the day's work.

The good weather held. We drove to Old Gentleman's house to find our crew ready to begin, even to fresh seaweed in the walks. I had a friend with me today. Years ago I learned to be grateful for small miracles and this one was an old friend from Hiroshima. Our acquaintance began when he and his wife and children came to the United States in connection with some of the young women who, as little girls, had been sadly wounded but not killed by the atomic bomb. While he traveled to give lectures and raise money for hospital expenses during the surgery necessary to restore their marred faces to something like their natural beauty, his wife and three children had spent the summer in my great house. I found him waiting for me that morning and it was cheering to see his friendly face.

"Would you like to go with me for today's shooting?" I asked.

There is of course something of the actor in every preacher. "What a pleasure," he said, his good face lighting.

As we drove to Old Gentleman's house we talked of many things. I learned that Hiroshima is rebuilt and much bigger than before, numbering now some half million souls, each with a body attached. I mention the body, because it was the body that was destroyed by the bomb, and bodies are valuable for it is through them alone, it seems, that souls can communicate.

The day passed at once too swiftly and too long. My Hiroshima friend stayed by me, absorbed in the infinite detail of making a motion picture. We talked now and again.

"Promise me that you will come to Hiroshima before you leave Japan," he begged.

I could not promise. I knew I would not go. It was not as if I were needed. The people of Hiroshima have lived through the disaster, they have learned that peace is the most valuable goal in human life, for unless there is peace there is death. If I should go to Hiroshima it would be as a sightseer, and I am not that—not in Hiroshima. But I could not explain all that to my friend.

We parted at the end of the day, he to return to his reborn city and I to my room. I was there and I was not there. In absolute rest I spent the evening in a silence which was only a step from sleep. Sometime in the night I was wakened by laughter under my window. I rose and looked out. The moon was shining again and there in the big pool three young men were bathing, their slim nude bodies half hidden in the steaming mists of the earth-heated water, a scene so beautiful with life that I was half convinced, as I watched, that the painter has the best of us all as artist.

It was the last day at Old Gentleman's house, and I was loath to leave. The farmhouse location had been delightful, and I had made friends with all the family there, even with the cock and his hens and the goat. Only with the barking pig did I maintain a certain distance, feeling a mutual lack of interest, a result, doubtless, of our having nothing in common.

With Old Gentleman's household I had much in common. I enjoyed to the full their cultivated minds, their delicate courtesy, their friendliness at once frank and restrained. Yet the end must come there, too. Old Gentleman had performed his part with dignity and grace, his servant had led young Yukio, the farm boy, and Toru, the fisherman's son, into the stately house and had led them to the gate again after Toru had made his fateful choice to leave. The servant had his great moment at that gate, for here it was that he had his momentous dialogue, his yes and his no. He spoke these two words with importance and indeed they are the most important words in any language, containing within their brief sounds the positive and negative forces of the entire universe.

We said our farewells, too, we bowed and gave thanks, and I signed hundreds I am sure, of the big autograph cards that are used for this purpose in Japan. It is almost a pleasure to write one's name on the ample cream-white surface, so exactly right for a brush or wide soft black lead. Instinctively one writes the name large and in graceful lines. The result is gratifying, somehow, and satisfaction is increased because of the silver edges of the handsome card and the silver stars sprinkled on the back.

Regretfully we gathered ourselves together and left the beautiful place and the kind people who live there and were conveyed by truck and car to our next location, the village of Kitsu. Our vehicles dislodged us on the top of a cliff and from there the approach was on foot and by a narrow path clinging to the rocky hillside. We walked down and down, until we came to the village itself, a cluster of stone cottages separated by narrow cobbled streets. I knew as I walked those streets that already I loved Kitsu the best of all our locations. A glorious bright day it was, the sun burning down upon the sand, and alas, this time the script called for rain. Rain had been forecast over the radio from Nagasaki, but rain there could not be from that brilliant blue sky. Therefore again we must make rain.

And we made rain all day and all night, it seemed, until we pumped the village well dry. The rain making was primitive but effective. A heavy canvas hose connected the well with the tank near the fisherman's house where the scene was to take place. The tanks were big wooden tubs, each holding fifty gallons of water but I do not know why we did not put the hose into the ocean, for fifty gallons is only a drop in what we needed. Each time that we were ready for the scene some-one shouted that the water had given out and the gasoline pump went to work again. Or when we were ready for the scene, actors in position and rain pouring, the make-up man discovered a hair out of place on our star's forehead, or a rill of sweat on his brow, and by the time that damage was mended, once more we had no more water and so no more rain.

Yet rain we continued to need for now came the scenes when Old Gentleman warned the fisherman's family that the big wave was sure to come. Grandfather cackled that there would be no typhoon, only rain. The village elders, locally provided extras and very proud of their new career, assembled on the narrow veranda of Toru's house and agreed with him.

Those elders! I did not imagine that one village could have provided such a collection of snaggle-toothed, cheerful, wise-cracking, withered old men, but Kitsu could, evidently, for there they were. At first they were preternaturally grave and well-behaved, especially one eagle-faced old bird of a man, who blinked his hooded eyes occasionally but otherwise gave no sign of life until the director requested some laughter at an appropriate moment. The old bird then staggered us all by shouting, in a stentorian bass voice, a string of words which when translated went thus:

"Put on your hat, American! That'll make me laugh!"

Everyone roared, for this hat had already become a joke. It was a small loosely braided straw, a bright sulphur-yellow, the crown encircled by a vivid variegated band. It was useful merely in locating the whereabouts of the director.

By the time we were really in action after the laughter, and at last synchronizing water with rain, a radio began to blare and again we stopped, the sound man in despair. The blast was from the school on top of the cliff, and the village headman, all devotion, raced up the mountain to make sure the children were clean and well-behaved. We waited and the water gave out, but the children arrived clean, their noses were wiped, and they were wearing clean cotton dresses or pants as the case might be. The headman was proud but stern. Left to themselves, he said, they would surround us and stifle activity. As it was, under his firm but benevolent discipline, however administered, they went about their daily work, obviously eaten up with curiosity about us, but subdued. He with the bowed legs bustled about, a human crab albeit a smiling one.

O Kitsu, darling village! I sat last night in a small empty theater in New York and looked at the finished picture, one friend beside me to share remembrance and to decide whether the picture is what we thought it was when we made it. Others must be the judges finally, for when Kitsu came back to me on the screen, when I saw the sea rolling in on the white beach, the many-colored nets hung there to dry, the boats at rest rising and falling gently on the waves, the noble rocky cliffs of shore and mountain and, yes, perhaps most of all, the fine good faces of the villagers, I felt a surge of spiritual homesickness. There are a few places, a few haunts, so natural to one's being that they are forever home. I do not know whether I shall ever see Kitsu again in this life, but it is with me and in me.

Let me remember!

From the top of the winding narrow path, as I first saw it, Kitsu is, as I have said, a cluster of roofs on a narrow neck of land cradled between the two arms of the sea, each roof as close to the next as the scales of a fish. From the sea it is different and from the sea I like it best. Each morning we climbed into boats harbored at Obama, we swept along the superb coastline for half an hour and then, rounding a high cliff above the massive rocks, we faced the white beach and the stone walls of Kitsu. Those houses had no windows to the sea. The people when they slept sought shelter from their powerful friend and enemy. The schism was obvious. They lived by the sea and would not live elsewhere, but the sea's mood was their mood. If the day dawned fair and windless, if the water was as blue as the Mediterranean, then the whole village was alive with laughter and business. If the sky was gray and the wind harsh, the people, unsmiling and anxious, crept along the sea walls to lash their boats firmly to the rocks they had rolled to the beach, and then crept back again into their houses. On a fair day if we entered the wide cove early we might be lucky enough to see the fleets of fishing boats putting out to sea and that was a sight to remember. On a stormy day the open waves broke into angry surf and we went by land. Sitting there in the dark theater in the center of a great American city, I returned to Kitsu. I saw Toru and Yukio in the boat fishing and Setsu—well, I must not tell the story. I see the children's faces, laughing and carefree, I see those same children grown, their young faces firm with will and purpose, Toru a young man declaring his love under the shelter of the great gray rocks at the end of the curving beach, twisted and hollowed by storm and wind.

Our days fell into the pattern of work. We rose early, breakfasted, and left the hotel at seven. A quarter of a mile away we took ship, and were carried swiftly to the village. Once there each person proceeded to his individual preparation for the day's scene. For an hour there was no need for me and I walked along the beach, past the stone break-water to the foot of a steep hill. Some steps led up this hill for an eighth of a mile or so, and at the top was a little empty stone temple, once a Shinto shrine. A low wall surrounded it, and the view was sea and mountains and sky.

I found my own niche, however, behind the shrine. At the edge of the high cliff there was a hollow in the rocks which exactly fitted my body. There I went every morning and, held in this hollow as though in his arms, I lay at rest. It was not the rest of sleep. It was the rest of the mind emptied, the spirit freed. He and I had never been here together. In the years when I had lived upon Kyushu I did not know that he existed, nor did he dream of me. Nor was there communication between us now—I cannot pretend that I heard his voice or even was aware of his presence. What did take place gradually as the days passed was a profound insurge of peace. No one became part of me, but I became part of the whole. The warm rock bed in which I lay, the wind rising cool from the sea, the sky intensely blue and the drifting white clouds, the gnarled pine tree bent above my head—of these I was a part, and beyond these, of the whole world. Myself ceased to be, at least for a time, a lonely creature with an aching heart. I was aware of healing pouring into me. It is a fact that at the end of the hour when the conch shell blew, I was able to rise refreshed to join my fellow workers.

The stone steps? I saw them again last night in the dark theater when Old Gentleman came down to warn the villagers, his faithful servant following. Yes, those are the same steps I climbed every morning, thirsting for the peace I found in the shelter of the rock. It became a habit, I woke eager for the hour and savored it deeply and with new zest each day. Then I discovered that something of each day's peace was left as residue for the night. I did not use it all up, there was an accumulation. I became stronger. I was able to miss a day, then two days, then more. Gradually I was established in myself and I needed no more to climb to that high lonely place and wait to receive. I was able to manufacture peace within myself merely by recalling the sweep of sea and mountain and sky and myself curled into the hollow rock. I had the peace inside me then, and the place became a shrine in my memory. I do not know how this healing came about. I did not pray, if prayer be words or pleading or searching. If the process must be explained, it was simply that I gave myself wholly to a universe which I do not understand but which I know is vast and beautiful beyond my comprehension, my place in it no more than a hollow in a rock. But there is the hollow and it is mine and there is the rock.

This chronicle, if it is to be worth anything, must be truthful. We were approximately one-fourth of the way through the making of the picture and we had arrived at the desert which lies in the middle half of every creative project. The desert begins at that point where progress is too far to consider giving up, and so far from completion that the end is invisible and can be contemplated only by faltering faith. How well I know the bleak prospect! I face it in every book I write. The first quarter of it goes like a breeze from the sea. The work is pure joy. It is sure to be the best book I have ever written. Then I enter upon the middle half of the book and joy departs. The characters refuse to move or speak or laugh or cry. They stand like pillars of salt. Why, oh, why was the book begun? Too much work has been done to cast it aside, yet the end is as far off as the end of a rainbow. There is nothing to do but plod ahead, push the characters this way and that, breathe on them hotly in the hope of restoring life, use every means of artificial respiration. Somewhere, some day, though it is unbelievable for weeks and months or even years, they do begin to breathe. What relief! The desert is past, the last quarter of the book breezes again.

On a morning in the middle of the desert period of the picture I sat on the edge of a fishing boat and watched our star, Sessue Hayakawa. With grim patience he was waiting to be called to the set. The scene had to be repeated because the sound man reported a fly on the microphone which nobody had noticed. There were flies in spite of the repellent which one of the crew sprayed zealously on the just and the unjust alike, and one fly had cunningly concealed himself on the microphone and buzzed enough to outsound everything else. Our star waited and his secretary-maid fanned him under his heavy robes.

"Why doesn't someone fan me so strategically?" the American director demanded.

No one answered and no one fanned him. Only the star sat patiently on. In his hand he held a tiny transistor radio. He was listening to a fight and when I smiled he explained that only thus could he find life endurable under the circumstances. Meanwhile, the make-up man ran to apply iced towels to his wrists and neck and to touch up his face and the star lit a large cigar to the infinite terror of the make-up man who feared for the beard he had so carefully applied. No one dared to suggest anything to the star, however, and he smoked in peace, his eyes closed as he listened to the fight.

On the set the director struggled with our grandfather, who though actually old, had too young a voice. The director illustrated how an old man's voice should sound. I held my peace. I know that old men's voices are high and shrill, not low and husky, but I held my peace. I had learned the first day to hold my peace—"for God's sake!"

Somehow we struggled through the middle desert, getting up early every morning, crowding exhausted into the boats at night, assuaged only by the beauty of the sunset sky. There were nights when we worked so late that it was dark when we took ship and the sea sparkled with tiny phosphorescent fish, outdoing the stars in the heavens.

And Sessue Hayakawa, advanced to the last day of his contract with us, was finishing his scenes as Old Gentleman and we were still in the desert. Make-up man had done rather a skillful job of aging him the ten years for which the script called, but the same wind which had made the surf too high for the boats one morning blew off his left eyebrow. Make-up man was fit to be tied, because he did not bring an extra eyebrow with him from the hotel. There was nothing to be done except to make an eyebrow from white hairs left over from the beard. . . . Everything continued to go wrong. The cakes the kindhearted citizens of the town left with us as a treat for the crew turned out to be of an undesirable variety and nobody would eat them. We were all morose. The rushes had been delayed that we hoped to see a week ago. A Japanese holiday had intervened, and a Sunday, and we had seen very few rushes, so that we were at least three days behind schedule. We drew apart and pondered dark thoughts. Could anybody understand the English our actors speak? We were trying the impossible—Japanese actors playing in English! Young Yukio and young Toru, our farm mother, among others, spoke little or no English, and now they spoke it, but was it good enough? How would it sound, even when our star spoke, to an American audience?

In the midst of the desert of pessimism we had a letter from our business manager in Tokyo. She had seen the rushes of Old Gentleman and they were superb, she said, including dialogue. They made her cry, she reported. For that young sophisticate to cry means something. We had not supposed it possible, so cool and collected was she, so chary of praise. Our hopes soared. Perhaps we were almost out of the desert.

In renewed spirits we gave a dinner for Sessue Hayakawa in honor of his leaving us. He was in a fine mood and drank a mixture of cold beer and saké, which he sustained admirably, and his stories were as good as his plays. Fifty years in theater in many countries made a lifetime of stories worth telling. We were sorry to see him go, and I think he was sorry to leave us, but there is nothing permanent in theater life. We work together closely for a few days and weeks and months, growing fond of one another, we part and forget. Nothing goes deep—it is the only way to bear it.

The rushes arived and we went to the theater across the street after the evening show was over. They did not make me cry but I was pleased with them. Then suddenly I saw our young star, our grown-up Toru. He was sitting in the row ahead of me, heavily asleep. My heart sank under the seat. Could he sleep? Yes, he could and did. I turned to my companion.

"Look at that!"

"He is drunk," was the indignant reply.

Yes, there was a party tonight and our young star was drunk. It was all too obvious when the rushes ended and we left the theater. He could not stand up. Nevertheless, I felt chilled. Drunk or sober, how could he sleep? No, we were still in the desert and we could only plod on.

There was one more moment in the day. It was the last glimpse, the final close-up, of Old Gentleman's servant. We took it in front of the hotel, and the crowd gathered, a prosperous holiday crowd with cameras and gaiety. Old Gentleman's servant was of course the little ancient wardrobe man but he had gained a new dignity. He had achieved a lifelong dream. He was now an actor. All these years he had only been making clothes and finding costumes for others to wear upon the stage. But now he had worn a costume of his own, he had had his face made up—only a little, for it was such a perfect face for the part. That night he stood in the presence of the crowd with calm and dignity and the cameraman took the close-ups we needed for the final film. When they were finished, we bowed and shook hands, we thanked him and he bowed in return. He told us that this was the greatest year of his life. He had become an actor, he had played a part with Sessue Hayakawa, and next month he was to marry off his daughter.

So the day ended.

"Otsukaresama!"

It is a word meaning, "You are tired," a gentle Japanese way of saying, "You may quit for the day."

It was true. We were tired.

We were now well past the desert. There was one big scene left for Kitsu, the coming of the tidal wave. While we had been working around this scene, our special-effects man had been creating it in the special-effects studio in Tokyo. Twice he had come to Obama to consult and to take hundreds of pictures of Kitsu and the empty beach beyond. We knew that we were in safe hands, the tidal wave would be perfect, but we could not see it until we returned to the city. Ours was the task of creating the approach to the wave, and the recovery from it.

An air of tensity and dread crept into the village as we prepared for the scene of the tidal wave. This was cutting near the bone. Every man, woman and child feared above all else in their beautiful precarious life the ungovernable tidal wave striking with no warning except the low and ominous roar over the horizon, the muddied water of the well, the quiver of the earth. Even to imagine the horror was almost more than they could bear as they set themselves doggedly to the task of acting the dread reality. Farm and fisher families played their parts well, and we drew near to the final evening, when in the darkness the torches flamed before Old Gentleman's house and the panic-stricken Kitsu families fled from their ancestral homes up the narrow winding mountain path to safety at the top of the cliff.

Toru was for that evening the star, the boy Toru. Our part of the scene was to bring him to the moment when he sees the village swept away, and we see it in his face. The tidal wave was to be inserted here and after it we took over again when Toru, in agony and madness and all but swept away himself, was saved only by a strong kind hand put out to seize him as he clung to the cliff. He acted the part superbly but I remember especially the people swarming up the hillside, the dogged frightened people taking the path their ancestors had trodden so often before them, but in reality.

That night when it was all over and we went away soberly, we gained a new understanding of the incomparable courage of the Kitsu folk, the unswerving devotion to the sea and to their way of life, a clean good way, but perilous. We said good-by with tender regret. I have memories of a crowd of kind faces in the lantern light, of the headman proudly receiving our praise and thanks, saying the only reward he wished was to know when the picture would be shown in Japan.

"We will put on our best clothes and go even to Tokyo," he told us.

At last on the mountain the flames of the torches at Old Gentleman's gate died into final darkness. It was over, the picture was made, and never shall I forget the long beautiful days of sea, wind and sunshine, of meals shared on the beach, and the great pewter pots of tea, nor shall I ever forget the hours of rest I spent lying half asleep in an empty boat drawn up on the shore, the drowsy sound of waves in my ears, the heat of noon upon me. I had put away in those days and for the time being the waiting shadows of loss and loneliness. I lived for the day, the hour, the work, the deep organic healing of the warmth of the sun, the driving rain, and the stormy sea.

We were so near the end of the picture now that we could plot the design of our days. After Kitsu came the empty beach of Chijiwa and here was the great shark-catching scene and the last scene with the children now grown and finding love and life, joy and sorrow. Last of all at Kitsu was the scene with Old Gentleman, Toru and Setsu. After that there remained only the volcano scene at Oshima to be shot and inserted at its proper place in the film.

I am going too fast. Let me remember first Chijiwa itself. In a crowded country, on a matchless shore, this wide and beautiful beach is left unpopulated. It is empty and has been for centuries. Go there any day and you will see fishing nets spread out to dry but no people. Chijiwa faces the sea at a peculiar angle so that typhoons and tidal waves strike it with a devastating force, and the fisherfolk, after the often repeated experience of total destruction, have listened at last to the threatening sea and live there no more.

It is a supremely fine beach, nevertheless, stretching two miles long and reaching deep into the land, its boundaries, east and west, huge and handsome rocks. My life in Asia and my love of Asian art has conditioned me to rocks. They add stability to the landscape, and the shapes they take from age and weather express the moods of nature. They signify strength and resistance and eternal values. At the far end of Chijiwa there were such rocks, and against them as backdrop we played the final love scene with Toru and Setsu, grown-up. It was toward the rocks Old Gentleman went when he bade them his last farewell.

Let me not forget, either, the sharks. It is a unique scene in the picture and it was a unique experience to perform. Once a year the fisherfolk of that region go out to hunt sharks. These cruel creatures of the sea destroy the fish in any area they choose to possess and fishermen make war against them. Their coming is heralded by shoals of small fish, the bait fish, and when these appear, the fishermen prepare their strategy. They bring their boats, some two hundred, and stretch between them the biggest net in the world and the strongest. Then the boats widen into a vast circle and as the bait fish swim into its space, the sharks follow. When the net is full of the squirming monsters the boats draw together and the sharks are in a trap. On the shore hundreds of men haul in the net, and drag the sharks to the beach. There they club the sharks to death, then cart them away, their tender parts to be eaten, the rest to be made into oil and fertilizer. Sometimes the take is good, sometimes it is not. Last year the men caught only one shark, but this year we brought them luck, they said, for they caught and killed one hundred and twenty.

I have no affection for sharks but I did not enjoy the clubbing. I did enjoy very much the fleet of fishing boats, their gay flags flying in the bright sunshine, and the lively crowd on the shore. The crowd was always with us, and long ago we had learned to accept them as part of the landscape. Why should I describe the scene further, when it is all there in the picture and better than I can tell it in words? It is an ancestral war, this, between man and shark, and on that day man won. And while the battle was being fought again, our characters carried on their own personal strife, the grown Haruko and Setsu in their memorable fight, when Haruko sought to drown Setsu, and Toru and Yukio, no longer children, faced the private dangers of being men. It is all there in the picture, even to the end when Toru sets out for sea in his boat and with his love.

We had now only to return to Oshima, yet I had one dream to fulfill. It was a small dream, of no importance to anyone except myself, and it was to go to the little Japanese house on the mountainside near Unzen where once in a previous life, I had taken refuge during the Second Revolution in China. The attacking army proved to be Communist-led, and all Westerners had been compelled to leave the city of Nanking where we were living. To Japan I had come with my family and a few other Americans and to the mountains above Nagasaki. Thither I returned now, with a Japanese friend as guide and interpreter.

We rented a car and driver and at the usual breackneck speed we wound our way along the abruptly curving road to Unzen. The mountain village I remembered had grown into a modern spa, but the hot springs were the same, spouting jets of steam from hundreds of small vents in the rocks, and people were boiling eggs and heating water for tea over the natural fires. I could not find my way through the new streets to the old country road I remembered, and we stopped a young woman to inquire if she had ever heard of houses where once, years ago, American refugees from China had lived. Her face lighted—yes, her grandfather knew and he had often spoken of those Americans. She produced the grandfather, a thin sprightly old man, who cheerfully led us to the road and down into a shallow valley, across a brook and up the mountain again until at last we came to the cluster of Japanese houses. They were empty now and closed, but I saw the little place of shelter where we had lived safely for a while and among friends but in great poverty, stripped by the revolution of all we had owned. My life had changed completely in the intervening years. I was no longer the rather desperate young woman who had lived under that roof and the overhanging pines. I pressed some money on the old man and went away, knowing I would never return. As we left Unzen, however, someone called us and we stopped the car. It was the young woman and she handed me a package.

"My grandfather says he remembers that you used to buy these rice cakes for your children," she said.

It was true. I had forgotten, but he had not.

Oshima had looked hellish enough on our scouting trip in May but now it was October and the volcano had been active and rebellious in the months between. Even in Tokyo the weather was ominous. We had planned to go by air and had chartered a plane that was to take us all across the channel in relays but the morning dawned somber and gray and the pilot refused to fly. We were working against time now, each of us anxious to get home or to overdue jobs, and to avoid delay we took passage on the night boat. A typhoon was in the offing and even a ship had its hazards. We had taken so many risks, however, had committed ourselves to sea and air so often, that one more risk seemed plausible.

In driving rain and howling wind we drove to the quay that night and boarded a top-heavy, old-fashioned steamer. Fortunate the darkness, for we could not see how many people were embarking. We got ourselves on board, camera, crew, actors and all, and went at once to our cabins. In a few minutes we were under way and heading for the sea.

I shudder as I remember that fearful night. The sea was vicious, the wind and rain contending enemies, but worst of all, the ship was carrying four times its proper load of passengers and again these passengers were hundreds of school children, off on an excursion to Oshima. They were seasick by the hundreds, poor little things, and the lavatories and corridors became unusable and impassable. The real danger, however, was in the ship itself. The superstructure was far too high and the vessel rolled from side to side to a degree that imperiled our lives. I am a seasoned sailor and have crossed oceans again and again from my first voyage across the Pacific at the age of three months to my last flight across the same ocean a few months ago at an age grown indefinite, yet never have I been in fear as I was that whole night long on the way to Oshima. Somewhere, before dawn, a friend who was traveling with us came in to see how his wife, my cabin mate, was faring. His good face was green with terror.

"We're breaking all the laws of mathematics," he groaned. "The ship is rolling at an impossible mathematical degree. It can't be done. We should by rights be flat on our side and floundering."

I lay on my berth and reflected upon a strange life—my own. How is it that a mild-mannered peaceable woman with no desire, ambition or even inclination for adventure manages somehow to be always in the midst of adventure? So passionately do I love the usual, the commonplace, the everyday, that I turn off the television instantly if an adventure program comes on. It is no use. I am contantly involved in some daring expedition and loathing it, and I have always particularly hated the thought of drowning at sea. I dislike drowning in any case, but if it must be my end I prefer a small swimming pool or better still, a bathtub. Yet I cannot count the seas I have traveled upon, how many times the Pacific, scarcely less often the Atlantic, the Mediterranean, the Red Sea, and all the seas curling in and around the complex shores of Asia. Now apparently I was to meet my fate between Tokyo and Oshima. The Big Wave, indeed!

Dawn came at last, a weak wet dawn, the pale sun fringed with mists, and the ocean still growling and snarling its white-crested waves in contradictory currents. The dim outlines of Oshima appeared from nowhere and we struggled into our clothes. In fifteen minutes we were due to dock. Fifteen minutes became an hour and then two hours while we continued to roll. We could not dock, it appeared, because the sea was too rough. If it did not subside, we were told, we would be compelled to go to the other side of the island where there was an inferior dock. It did not subside and we went to the other side of the island to the inferior dock. A long procession of pale but determined school children disembarked and then we got off and went through rain to the hotel. This time I was too subdued to protest when I found myself again quartered in the Emperor's room, a setting I had refused on my earlier visit as being too overwhelming for the modest citizen of a republic.

We had a quick breakfast and set out by car to the foot of the volcano. There horses waited for those who wanted to ride. I chose to walk, for it had been some years since I had been on horseback. Moreover experience had taught me to distrust the Asian horse, mule or pony. They lead a hard life, for the Asian is not sentimental about animals, as we Americans are. The philosophy of the transmigration of souls leads the Asian to believe that the human being who has been criminal in life will in his next phase be an animal not to be trusted to behave better than the criminal who inhabits him. While I cannot say that I believe this, yet if I were to judge by the behavior of horses I have known in Asia, I might at least consider it possible that they are indeed animated by some evil force. "Put not your trust in horses," the good book tells us. On foot, therefore, I climbed the black volcano, ascending a dark and barren landscape spectacularly, horrifyingly beautiful.

Under a stormy gray sky the effect was even more somber and strange. Streamers of white steam flew from every crack and cranny of the volcano and the surrounding high mountains. These I had not seen on my previous visit, and were to be explained by the typhoon, I found upon inquiry. The crater of the volcano is very large, and had in the last few days become larger, for under the torrential rains the walls had crumbled at various places. Wherever there was a surface it had been dampened and choked and the steam thus held back had forced its way through channels in the mountains. Hence the ribbons and banners of steam, all blown by the wind in one direction. Again and again I stopped on my way to look at the spectacle, for spectacle it was. I have seen some of the most magnificent scenery in the world, but for splendor and terror, I put first the volcano on Oshima island, that day.

Two days we spent there, reckless, wonderful, unforgettable days. Only a short time before we came the volcano had erupted, throwing great rocks into the air and gnawing at the mountain. Guards stood everywhere now to forbid us passage, but we pushed our way to the very edge of the crater in spite of them, the camera perched precariously anywhere it could stand or be held. The drop into the crater was at two levels, the one an encircling terrace, the other without bottom and hidden in clouds of vile-smelling gas and steam. Camera and crew and director descended to the terrace, but I stayed at the edge above, not only because I am prudent, but because the distracted guards warned us that we must all run for our lives if we heard the slightest roar or rumbling from inside the crater. I did not wish to imperil the young men, in such case, who might feel in honor compelled to run at my slower pace.

The wind blew bitterly cold and work went on without the usual laughter and good cheer. Swiftly and with concentration each did his part. I confess my heart lost too many beats as I watched the crew walking about inside the crater, leaping across great cracks, sinking into soft ashy soil, standing at the very edge of the abyss. I recalled it all again when the rushes were shown in the theater in New York. I saw the boy Yukio standing there on the screen, his eyes wide with fear, the white steam curling upward from the crater and enclosing him. No wonder he cries out to his father,

"We are unlucky, we people of Japan!"

"Why do you say that?" his father asks.

"Sea and the mountain," the boy says, "they work to destroy us."

We were glad when the two days were ended, the work finished, and yet we would not have missed the experience. I shall never forget the landscape, black as the other side of the moon. And we flew across the water on the third day under a clear sky and arrived at Tokyo airfield in exactly forty-five minutes, safely.

Five days later the volcano went into eruption and the lava-black soil upon which we had stood fell into the abyss.

So the picture was made. It was finished except for the scene of the tidal wave, which was being built in the special-effects studio in Tokyo. Thither I went on my last day. The famous special-effects artist was waiting for me, debonair in a new light suit and hat and with a cane. He had the confident air of one who knows that he has done a triumphantly good job, and after a survey of the scene I agreed with him. In a space as vast as Madison Square Garden in New York, which is the biggest place I can think of at the moment, he had reconstructed Kitsu, the mountains and the sea. The houses were three feet high, each in perfect miniature, and everything else was in proportion. A river ran outside the studio and the rushing water for the tidal wave would be released into the studio by great sluices along one side. I looked into the houses, I climbed the little mountain, I marveled at the exactitude of the beach, even to the rocks where in reality I had so often taken shelter. The set was not yet ready for the tidal wave. That I was to see later on the screen in all its power and terror. I had seen everything else, however, and I said farewell, gave thanks, and went away.

My hotel room had become a sort of home, and I felt loath to leave it, yet I knew that my life in it was over. It had been a pleasant place and I had lived there in deepening peace. Now the old dread of facing another life without him and of returning alone to the places where we had always been together was with me again. It had to be done, however. I could not escape, and there could be no further postponement.

"Come back, come back soon to Japan," my dear friends said, and I promised that I would and, tearing myself away, I went alone into the jet plane that was to carry me back again to New York.

I say New York, although of course New York is only on the way to my farmhouse home in Pennsylvania. But I have a stopping place in New York, that city of wonders and grief. He and I always kept a place there. He needed it for his work and for his spirit, and I have continued our tradition. It is not the same place we shared for so many years. Within the confines of our old apartment I could not escape the torture of memory. Whether I would have stayed I do not know, but the skyscrapers of steel and glass had pushed their way up our avenue, and the building in which we had made a city home was to be torn down. I found a place farther uptown in a new building, where there were no memories except the ones I carry hidden wherever I am.

And here I tell a story that has nothing to do with the picture, except that it provides a closing scene for myself. When I was looking for the new apartment a daughter helped me by sorting out the impossibles and bringing me at last to see the two or three possibles. It was night, I remember, when I looked at these places. I was in haste and it did not seem to matter much where I lived. We entered bare unpainted rooms. I saw a wide window and through the darkness I discerned dimly a building whose roof faced my window, a school, my daughter said, and fortunate for me, for there would be no high building to cut off the view. I did not care very much about that, either, for when do I have time in New York to look at a view? Besides, I have plenty of view in my Pennsylvania home. So I decided upon impulse.

"I'll take it."

The choice was haphazard, I would have said, a chancy thing. But I am beginning to believe that there is no such thing as pure chance in this world. For here is the preliminary to this closing story:

When I was a child and often reluctant to do my duty, my father used to say to me firmly but gently,

"If you will not do it because it is right, then do it for the greater glory of God."

For the greater glory of God then, and for my father's sake, though still reluctant, I did do what had to be done, at least as often as possible.

Now to return to the apartment. I did not once see it while it was being decorated. When all was finished I opened the door and went straight to the big window. It was a bright day, I remember, one of New York's best, the air fresh from the sea and the sky blue. And facing me, across the building, under the eaves and along the roof, I saw these words carved in huge stone letters:

AD MAIOREM DEI GLORIAM

They face me now as I write. To the greater glory of God! What does it mean, this voice from the grave, my father's grave? He lies buried on a mountaintop in the very heart of a China lost to me. I am here and alive and thousands of miles away. Are we in communication, he and I, through my father? It is not possible.

How dare I say it is not?

Some day we shall know. What day? That day, perhaps, when saints and scientists unite to make a total search for truth. It is the saints, the believers, who should have the courage to urge the scientists to help them discover whether the spirit continues its life of energy when the mass we call body ceases to be the container. Faith supplies the hypothesis, but only science can provide the computor for verification. The unbeliever will never pursue the search. He is already static, a pillar of salt, forever looking backward.

There are no miracles, of that I am sure. If one walks on water and heals the sick and raises the dead to life again, it is not a matter of magic but a matter of knowing how to do it. There is no supernatural; there is only the supremely natural, the purely scientific. Science and religion, religion and science, put it as I may, they are two sides of the same glass, through which we see darkly until these two, focusing together, reveal the truth.

On the day when the message comes through from over the far horizon where dwells "that great majority," the dead, the proof will reach us, not as a host of angels in the sky but as a wave length recorded in a laboratory, a wave length as indisputable and personal as the fingerprint belonging to someone whose body is dust. Then the scientist, recognizing the wave length, will exclaim, "But that's someone I know! I took his wave length before he died." And he will compare his record with the wave length just recorded and will know that at last a device, a machine, is able to receive a message dreamed of for centuries, the message of the continuing individual existence, which we call the immortality of the soul.

Or perhaps it will not be a scientist who receives, but a woman, waiting at a window open to the sky.